Wizards

of

Wall Street

By Zubi Diamond

Copyright © Zubi Diamond 2009

Zubi Diamond
Published by Diamond Publishing
www.zubidiamond.com

Library of Congress Cataloging-in-Publication Data

Table of Contents

i

Introduction

Economic crisis 101
The scam that elected Barack Obama

This book will validate your suspicion of Washington DC government officials, lobbyist and Wall Street manipulators. It's got the beef in it. And because of the fragile economy, ballooning debt and 9 trillion dollars in deficit, and still counting, an administration that is clueless and the impending catastrophe; this is the most important book that everyone should read.

If you loved America and capitalism before the economic crisis hit and you wish that the crisis, the calamity never occurred, you should read this book.

If you were perplexed, confounded and befuddled about the reason for the economic crisis, this book offers the only logical credible explanation, and the only truth about what caused the economic crisis and the solution for fixing it without any more stimulus government spending; not one more dime of the American taxpayer's money is needed to fix this economic crisis.

This book contains the truth every American must know and the urgency to save our country from irreparable ruin. The economic crisis was deliberately engineered for profit and political gain.

The author has employed a great deal of passion and honesty into this incredible book. He has revealed the real criminals on Wall Street and in Washington DC. The people, who, as a consequence of their behavior and actions, have caused the economic crisis and are still digging America deeper into debt unless their dirty secret is revealed; What is in this book is the shocking truth. It is brutally honest. Find out who is looting America, destroying capitalism and introducing socialism.

This book offers the road map for a Republican comeback If President Obama fails to do the right thing.

Wizards of Wall Street

SECURA GROUP OF LECG

CHAIRMAN

THE HONORABLE BILL ISAAC.

Dear Mr. Isaac,

Yesterday, March 12, 2009, during the sub committee hearing on mark-to-market accounting, Congresswoman Marcy Kaptur from Ohio, asked you a series of rhetorical questions in amazement as to why the regulators and legislators were not moving swiftly to solve the problems created by the mark-to-market accounting. Then she also asked you what you would say to President Barack Obama if he was in the room with you, on how to fix this economic crisis.

Please allow me.
I want to answer those questions with a modified version of the letter I sent to the house financial services committee.

The reason why there has not been any previous movement to correct this mark-to-market accounting regulatory error was because of the extensive influence of Managed Funds Association, (MFA) a lobbying organization for the Hedge Fund short sellers.
They had already lobbied everyone that mattered, and got their support, so they had no opposition except you.

They are relentless, formidable, and well organized. They owned the stock markets during the tenure of Christopher Cox as the Chairman of the Security and Exchange Commission (SEC), and they still own it now. The SEC is supposed to be an independent regulatory body; but that is no longer the case; it is now controlled by Managed Funds Association. We need to wrestle the control of the stock market and our national economy from their greedy paws.

Through legislation, the American public, common investors, and equity shareholders, can reclaim the control of the stock market and our national economy from the greedy bear paws of Managed Funds Association members, to save capitalism and restore investor confidence. This must be done for our country, for duty and for honor.

Managed Funds Association lobbies every policy maker and regulatory body in Washington DC. They are very cunning and crafty; facilitated by their fundraising and campaign donations, they have been systematically misinforming, misdirecting and misleading regulators and policy makers for years. Their lies are made palatable by campaign contributions and fundraisers They lobbied the SEC, and the Financial Accounting Standards Board (FASB) to change the rules that created this mess; the economic crisis. They lobbied for the adoption of mark-to-market accounting regulation. And I am here to tell you that mark-to-market accounting regulation is a scam.

It is a fraudulent business scheme plotted by the Hedge Fund short sellers and their lobbyist to defraud the banking industry, and their shareholders, and defraud America in the process, promulgated by Christopher Cox through the Financial Accounting Standard Board and FAS 157.

I will explain it all to you. I will explain how and why they did it. Just keep reading. The plot thickens.

Christopher Cox devoted his tenure at the SEC to provide for and protect the Hedged fund short sellers, who are being represented by Managed Fund Association.

All the SEC new regulations and changes under Christopher Cox were put in place to favor managed funds association members at the expense of the common investors, the equity shareholders, 401k investors, mutual funds investors and individual retirement accounts.

A great deal of capital has been lost and destroyed with the financial market collapse.
Thus there is fear and lack of confidence among investors.

Recently, Barack Obama met with the House financial services committee Chairman, Barney Frank and ranking member Spencer Bachus, and said that he wants to come up with a new banking, or financial regulatory reform to protect investors.

Please make sure that any new financial regulatory reform protects the real investors and not the Hedge Fund short sellers and their broker dealers; by doing all of the following:

(1) Reinstate the uptick rule
(2) Remove mark-to-market accounting and replace it with historic cost accounting
(3) Dismantle and discontinue trading on all the short Exchange Traded Funds (ETFs), also called leveraged inverse ETFs.
(4) Reinstate the circuit breakers and the trading curb to kick in whenever the Dow Jones industrial average drops 150 points.
(5) Regulate the Hedge Funds just like you do mutual funds and pension funds.
(6) Regulate speculation on crude oil futures by banning margin and leveraging except for the airline industry or any other end user that can actually take delivery of the commodity.

The real investors that need to be protected by any new banking and financial regulatory reform are the stock equity shareholders, the ordinary public investors, the government worker investors, the American families, consumers, 401k employee investors, retirement portfolios, retired grand mother and grandfather investors, mutual funds investor, ordinary private citizen investors, pension funds investors at large. And not the Hedge Fund short sellers whom Christopher Cox during his tenure protected to the extent of destroying America and capitalism, due to their lobbying influence.

The regulatory mistakes of Christopher Cox is the reason why we are in this economic crisis, and any new banking, financial regulatory reform should aim to correct those mistakes.

All the regulatory mistakes made by Christopher Cox were lobbied for, by Managed Funds Association.

Managed Fund Association members, are all Hedge Fund short sellers.

The case against Christopher Cox and the lobbying influence of Managed Funds Association - the Hedge Fund short sellers, is as follows:

This economic crisis and stock market crashes are caused by two major regulatory mistakes made by Christopher Cox at the security and exchange commission. And the solution to fixing this economic crisis is to correct those mistakes. It is just that simple.

The two regulatory mistakes are namely
    (1) The removal of the uptick rule and
    (2) The introduction of mark-to-market accounting.

On July 6, 2007, Christopher Cox removed the uptick rule. The uptick rule is a safeguard regulation that governs short sale transactions, designed to prevent manipulation by short sellers from being able to force share prices downward, causing panic share declines.
Today, that downward pressure is being put on stocks through manipulation by Hedge Fund short selling; unrestricted Hedge

Fund short selling augmented with computerized program-short selling causing panic share declines and panic sell offs; our stock market is crashing every day.

On July 1st 2008, Christopher Cox, through FASB, introduced an unnecessary new accounting regulation FAS 157 called mark-to-market accounting. This added fuel to the fire. Mark-to-market accounting enormously exacerbated the economic decline and turned a would be normal slow down, before a continued growth and expansion, into a meltdown. It created a disaster that forced the financial institutions to mark down (mark-to-market) all their assets; consequently, it devalued their balance sheets with a continuous and indefinite perpetual write downs, coupled with Hedge Fund short sellers, bear raiding all the publicly traded company's stocks, because of the removal of the uptick rule. The removal of the uptick rule granted the Hedge Fund short sellers the license to raid, destroy and create havoc on these companies. They also created margin calls, credit rating down grades, liquidity crisis, credit crunch, lending freeze, run on banks and bankruptcies. Consequently, the bear raid resulted in the collapse of several financial institutions along with our national economy.

The removal of the uptick rule left the financial institutions vulnerable, and facilitated a bear raid on their company stocks, making it impossible for them to manage their investment risks and eventually causing them to collapse. (Investment risks meaning risky investments, including sub prime loans).

All the financial institutions that are already destroyed, every publicly traded company whose market cap is being destroyed and trillions of dollars in losses by American families and investors could have been prevented if the uptick rule had been left intact as a safeguard regulation and mark-to-market accounting had never been introduced, even though there were other issues like missteps by some corporate executives, missteps by some lawmakers, negative impact of community redevelopment act, and sub prime toxic mortgage papers.

The economy would have survived all these blunders if Christopher Cox had not removed all the safeguard rules that protected our economic system and financial markets, and broke down the underpinnings of capitalism.

It is time for the Congress and the Senate to call Christopher Cox and ask him some serious questions about the decisions he made at the SEC, and verify the truthfulness of his answers, the truthfulness of his previous testimonies and public statements on his reason for removing the uptick rule, and introducing mark-to-market accounting.

Today the government is confused, adopting extreme measures, throwing money at the symptoms of the crisis, and incredibly missing to kill the virus that is eating away at our financial markets, our economic stability, and our national security and investor confidence.

Any buy and hold investment in the stock market nowadays, would be destroyed by short sellers. Short selling in itself, is not the problem. The problem is the removal of the uptick rule, a safeguard regulation that governs short selling, which the security and exchange commission erroneously removed due to the Hedge Fund lobbying influence.

The removal of the uptick rule has rendered useless all the fundamental attributes of a company. It does not matter whether or not a company has a good balance sheet, or if the company is profitable, short sellers can target and evaporate the company in a matter of weeks. Buy and hold investment is dead.

Christopher Cox has turned the stock market into a casino, by removing the uptick rule and establishing leveraged inverse ETFs, where the Hedge Fund short sellers are the house and they determine if the market goes up or down by collusion. Every other person that dares to participate is a gambler, and the house always wins.

The Hedge Fund short sellers are making money on the backs of regular investor shareholders and retirement portfolios, pension funds and mutual fund shareholders and 401k employees.

The combination of removing the uptick rule and introducing mark-to-market accounting by Christopher Cox broke down the underpinnings of capitalism; it broke down the underpinnings of our economic and financial system and is routinely destroying capitalism and quickly introducing socialism to deal with the symptoms of his wrong doings.

Christopher Cox will tell you he performed some tests before removing the uptick rule, but I am here to tell you that the test was both unnecessary and inaccurate. It did not include a 'stress test.' It was done in a bull market and not in a volatile market, the Hedge Fund short sellers that lobbied for it just laid low in wait while the test was in progress, waiting to strike when all was clear. (When the test period was over and the rules had been changed).
Christopher Cox will also tell you that recent studies done to reinstate the uptick rule concluded that it is impossible due to operational issues at the brokerages. That is also not true. What Christopher Cox is alluding to, are the short ETFs, leveraged inverse ETFs, which he allowed the Hedge Funds short sellers and their broker dealers to establish, to further sink their hooks deeper into the controls of the market, to negate and circumvent the uptick rule, in case a new administration wants to reinstate the uptick rule. A simple solution to correct these operational difficulties at the brokerages will be for the SEC to halt trading on all the short ETFs without warning to prevent cheating and fraud, and settle every account at the last price traded.

The SEC need to dismantle all the short ETFs because it is a great source of massive stock market volatility and stock price manipulation, responsible for the daily destructions of bank stocks equity capital, and financial stocks equity capital, and any other publicly traded company or sector they choose to wreck.

Christopher Cox claims that he had an emergency temporary ban on short selling shares of financial companies from September 18th 2008 to October 8th 2008. But I am here to tell you that Christopher Cox was influenced by the Hedge

Fund lobby that he was just playing a shell game with the temporary ban on short selling in financial stocks, because short selling in itself is not the problem. The problem is the removal of the uptick rule, a safe guard regulation that governs short selling which the Hedge Fund lobby, lobbied Christopher Cox to remove.

While the temporary short selling ban on financial stocks was in effect, as Christopher Cox wants you to believe, the Hedge Fund short sellers moved their shorting activities to the financial ETFs, financial indexes, and other sectors. Yes, they continued shorting financial stocks through the ETFs, continued driving down the share prices of every company including financial stocks, and they colluded not to buy any stocks while the ban was in effect, so they can say to the Treasury Secretary Henry Paulson, you see " We are not the problem, short selling is not the problem, because all the financial stocks were still going down when the ban was in effect". But we know that as soon as the ban was lifted, they severely crashed the market in two days.

Christopher Cox also claims that investors support his decision to remove the uptick rule and that investors also support his adoption of the mark-to-market accounting rule, but this is not true either, because nefarious Hedge Fund short sellers are not investors, they are corporate looters. Christopher Cox does not seem to know the difference between investors, and Hedge Fund short sellers who lobbied him to change the rules.

To be an investor is to spend your hard earned money to buy an asset and commit capital in expectation of a future price appreciation and increase in value. Hedge Fund short sellers do not want price appreciation or increase in value, they only want and have an expectation of a future price decline and decrease in value leading to the destruction of the companies.

Hedge Fund short sellers are not investors; they are masquerading as investors, they are the proverbial wolves in sheep's clothing; they are the financial market looters, selling what they never owned and stealing what they never owned, because that is what short selling allows them to do. Short selling allows them the ability to sell shares of companies in which they are not stockholders or shareholders, and have never bought the stock or bought a share in the company. They are not investors; they just borrow the shares but the shares are never delivered; they are never in possession of the stock nor do they own it, yet they are able to sell it. They are not investors. They are not real investors.

Without the uptick rule as a safeguard and restriction that governs short selling, selling what you do not own by the Hedge Fund short sellers becomes abusive as they manipulate stock prices and overwhelm the market, putting downward pressure on stocks, causing panic share declines followed by company destruction and collapse, and frequent stock market crashes. Hedge Fund short sellers are not investors, they are destroyers and looters.

Investors are the public, the American families, the 401k employees, your retired grandmother, father and relatives, the government workers, ordinary private citizens, pension fund and mutual fund investors, all of whom had invested money in a fundamentally sound American company or companies in hope of a future price appreciation and increase in value. These people were led to believe you can plan your retirement and invest in conservative and fundamentally sound American companies, all of whom, their nest eggs have now been stolen and wiped out by the nefarious Hedge Fund short sellers. Those innocent investors are the real investors, the common investors and not the Hedge Fund short sellers who did the stealing, and took everybody's money. We are talking about looting all the financial institution's money and every body's 401k money in excess of 11 trillions dollars. Again, these Hedge Funds short sellers are not investors, they are looters.

These nefarious Hedge Fund short sellers are who Christopher Cox has sided with and is protecting, and facilitating their looting of America, the destruction of capitalism and our economy and national security.

Christopher Cox has totally lost track and contradicts the mission of the SEC which is to protect investors, maintain fair, orderly and efficient markets. And not protect the interests of Managed Funds Association members, the Hedge Fund short sellers and their broker dealers.

The Government, not knowing the truth about what happened, not knowing the truth about what caused the economic crisis, not knowing the truth about the looting of America, is still lost and confused, still handing out money, making bridge loans, and approving gigantic stimulus packages, working real hard in trying to replace all the money that was looted by the Hedge Fund short sellers. No amount of money or stimulus package will end this economic crisis until Congress and the Senate corrects the errors of Christopher Cox, which will not cost us any money.

Again, Congress, the Senate, or the White House can end this economic crisis by correcting the errors of Christopher Cox and that will not cost the tax payers any more money at all, nada, zero, zilch. Not one more penny will need to be spent to fix this economic crisis if Congress, The Senate or White House will do following:
- Reinstate the uptick rule.
- End mark-to-market accounting.
- End trading on all the short ETFs.
- Regulate the Hedge Funds like mutual funds and pension funds. Reinstate the circuit breakers.
- Regulate speculation in crude oil futures.

The government should correct the mistakes of Christopher Cox instead of wasteful stimulus packages and taxing the so-called rich, redistributing income, making Bridge loans to the banks, and re-capitalizing the banks.

Question:
- Has anyone asked what happened to the bank's capital that we now have to re capitalize them?
- What happened to the bank's money that they now need a bail out?

- What happened to all the money that these businesses lost?
- Where did the money go?
- Did the money vanish in thin air?
- Who has their money?

Answer. The Hedge Fund short sellers have the bank's money and everybody's money.

Christopher Cox has betrayed America; he has totally lost track and contradicts the mission of the SEC, which is to protect investors, maintain fair, orderly and efficient markets, and not to aid the Hedge Fund short sellers to orderly and efficiently loot money from the investors-shareholder class and all Americans. Christopher Cox has led the regular investors to their financial ruin; he has led the regular common investor to their slaughter.

Were the errors of Christopher Cox, just a bad regulatory decision or did something more sinister and nefarious occur?

The Hedge Fund short sellers are well organized.
They have a national association and trading organization.
They have Washington lobbyists (MFA). They do political fundraisers. They have media spokespersons; a propaganda unit; they understand the power of the media. They have regularly sent their representatives to different television stations to saturate the airwaves with misinformation and disinformation regarding this economic crisis. They have suppressed the truth about what caused the economic crisis; and have spread the blame for this crisis to every American except themselves.
Hedge Fund short sellers, through their media spokespersons; the propaganda team, have blamed the bankers, the lenders, the insurance companies, the borrowers, the Congress, the Senate, Barney Frank, Chris Dodd, Republicans, Democrats, sub prime mortgages, Sarbanes-Oxley, President Reagan, poor people, trickle-down economics, corporate executives, Alan Greenspan, the repeal of Glass Steagall Act, Community Redevelopment Act, Wall Street executives, bank CEOs,

President Carter, President Clinton, and President Bush for wanting every American to achieve their dream of home ownership. They have blamed our economic system. They said that every thing is too expensive, home prices and stock prices were too expensive, that we have borrowed too much money and people were playing musical chairs of borrowing, hoping that the music doesn't stop when it is their turn; leaving them stuck with a huge debt. They said that people are borrowing money from their homes and living off their home equity. The Hedge Fund short sellers have blamed every body for this economic crisis except themselves.

They are in essence blaming Americans for being Americans and living their blissful lives, playing by the rules and living within the law. They are blaming Americans for their lifestyle and capitalism, just like the terrorists do.

The Hedge Fund short sellers, through their media spokespersons are presenting themselves as smart and prudent, while the victims of their crimes: the bankers, regular investors, 401k investors, home loan consumers, mutual fund and pension fund investors are portrayed as stupid, unwise and lacking in good judgment.

But they did not mention their behind the scene lobbying activities to cheat and secretly change the rules of the game in the middle of the game. They did not mention how they secretly circumvented and removed the existing laws to cheat and gain advantage, making every law abiding citizen who was playing by the rules look stupid.

They also did not mention their behind the scene successful lobbying activities to subvert the system and impair and undermine the system by removing the safeguard rules that made the system called capitalism work for every American consumers and investors.

They did not tell you their behind the scene successful lobbying activities to remove the safeguard regulations that protected risk taking, protected investors and their invested capital, or prevented stock price manipulation and panic share declines.

They did not tell you their behind the scene successful lobbying activities to remove all safeguard regulation designed to protect Capitalism, to protect our financial institutions and all the publicly traded companies and their shareholders.

They did not tell you about their behind the scene successful lobbying activities to impair and undermine the banks and financial institutions by bringing back old regulations that were previously suspended because it had impaired the banks and caused several bank failures, leading to the Great Depression and the great Stock Market Crash of 1929.

They have conveniently failed to mention to you, where the $11 trillion dollars lost by American families, American businesses, American banks, investors, and retirement accounts and 401k accounts went to, and who has the money?

I am here to tell you all about that, to give you the missing piece of the puzzle that has confounded every one, every economist including Alan Greenspan. The missing piece that has the Government confused resulting in wasteful stimulus packages, bridge loans and bail outs, perpetuating the looting of America.

I do believe that Congress and the Senate really need to understand the whole truth about what has happened to our country, our financial markets, the greed that led to removing the safeguards of capitalism and the introduction of systemic destruction of equity capital and the demise of capitalism. All these issues, combined together, were brought to bear down and destroy our financial markets, our national economy and investor confidence by the actions of Christopher Cox with his removal of the uptick rule and his introduction of mark-to-market accounting due to the influence of the Hedge Fund lobby called Managed Funds Association, also known as the Hedge Fund short sellers.

The more you understand how this crisis was created, and all the related subject matters and issues, the better you will be prepared for any hearings related to this economic crisis and the better you will be prepared and ready to formulate and frame your questions for the witnesses, especially the follow-up questions that you would have to ask a witness when they give you an unsatisfactory answer, if you are in a quest for the truth, the search for the truth, regarding this economic crisis, how it was created and how to solve it, in order to revive America and Capitalism and restore investor confidence, and restore and fortify our economy, and national security.

The late Milton Friedman, the renowned economist, in his book, *A Monetary History of United States*, written in 1963, explained the reason for the Great Depression, and the 1929 stock market crash: He said that it was bad government regulations and bad monetary policy that caused the depression which led to the stock market crash. Regarding the reason why several banks failed in the 1930 era, he wrote, I paraphrase "The reason for several bank failures during the Great Depression was the decline in the short term market value of the bank's bond portfolio due to forced asset sale that brought down the value of good assets, as well as bad assets."

That, to me, sounds like the same effect of a mark-to-market accounting. "The forced sale of bond assets brings down the value of good bond assets as well as bad bond assets."

Of course, it is mark-to-market. They had mark-to-market accounting for eight years during the Great Depression, until 1938 when it was removed.

President Roosevelt suspended mark-to-market accounting in 1938, and it was replaced with a historic cost accounting model; a generally accepted accounting principle. (GAAP)

Today, the forced sale of a financial asset is bringing down the value of all similar assets held at all financial institutions because of the newly adopted accounting regulation called mark-to-market.

All similar assets are marked down to the last price sold or the current price, including long term assets like mortgage backed securities that may not be intended for sale, they are all now, being marked down to a short term market value and that deteriorates the bank's balance sheet, and is destroying capital and capitalism. And that coupled with Hedge Fund short sellers bear raiding the bank stocks, resulted in bank failures, and the subsequent stock market crashes and the slide towards the cliff's edge of a depression.

As I review the history of what caused the Great Depression and the 1929 stock market crash and noticing all the similarities with our own current economic crisis, noticing how a government agency, the SEC under Christopher Cox was influenced by the Hedge Fund short sellers' lobby to change the regulation to trigger this crisis.
I have come to the conclusion that:
This economic crisis is a manufactured crisis. It is artificial, and man made. It is deliberately engineered.
A crime has been committed.

(1) Why is Christopher Cox removing all the safeguard rules that were put in place to prevent a repeat of the 1929 stock market crash?
(2) Why did he bring back a previously suspended accounting regulation that was removed for having caused several bank failures in the past, which lead to the Great Depression and the Stock Market Crash of 1929? Why did he bring it back?

The Hedge Fund short sellers are well educated, and they do a lot of research before taking a short position. The expectation of any short position is to have a price decline; a huge price decline is always preferred. Consequently, Hedge Fund short sellers do relish a stock market crash. They want the market to crash. They love the market to crash.
 And, they have read Milton Friedman's book, a monetary history of the United States.
They knew the reason why the market crashed in 1929.They knew the reason why several banks failed in 1929.
They lobbied Christopher Cox to remove all the safeguard rules that were put in place to prevent a similar market crash from occurring. They lobbied Christopher Cox to change the accounting regulation to create conditions akin to 1929 that triggered several bank failures. And Christopher Cox said, yes, yes, and yes.

Our free and fair market is no more. The system is now broken. The market is now broken.

Christopher Cox, from the time he became chairman of the SEC was a friend to the Hedge Fund lobby, after all, the lobbyists are his former colleagues, Some of them were the toughest critics of the Hedge Fund industry, whom were hired off the house of Congress, and paid millions of dollars to lobby on behalf of the Hedge Fund short sellers.

Before Christopher Cox was appointed to the SEC, his predecessor was a Republican, Billionaire, William Donaldson, a very competent SEC chairman with practical Wall Street experience, who understood the market, the dynamics and who is who, and who are the Investors, and who are the opportunistic vultures. Chairman Donaldson abruptly resigned his position, after 2 years of major reforms, and some notable clashes and criticism from fellow Republican SEC board members, for being too tough on Wall Street, and the Hedge Fund industry, for wanting them regulated.
Unfortunately, the good guy left, leaving us to the mercy of, the incompetent and gullible fools. The facilitating tools of the looting Hedge Fund short sellers.

What ever the Hedge Funds short sellers wanted, Christopher Cox gave it to them. Their greed crashed the stock market. Their greed took down the economy and the country, and not the bankers.

They lobbied Christopher Cox to set up inverse leveraged ETFs, so they can circumvent the uptick rule and manipulate the markets, he complied.

They lobbied him to remove the uptick rule, a safeguard regulation that governs short sale transaction. He complied.

They asked him to discard the circuit breaker, and trading curb because they were out dated. He complied.

The Hedge Funds short sellers owned the market under Christopher Cox.

They were bear raiding companies at will, shorting stocks fearlessly without an uptick, colluding to determine the direction of the market. They traded fearlessly without risk, and transferred all the fear, and risk of investment losses and capital losses to the regular investors - shareholders. They were causing massive volatility and panic share declines. They were looting America.

(They will send their representative to testify in your house financial services sub committee hearing and other hearings, to tell you how to better regulate them, how to tackle the current crisis. do not listen to him - the representative. he is the enemy. put him in hand cuffs).

These Hedge Fund short sellers being the opportunists, and the vultures that they are, when they thought that there could be problems with sub prime mortgages, and securitization in structured finance, and knowing the bank's vulnerability with those asset quality, shorted the bank's stocks and the financial institution's stocks and focused on them as their main target for a major take down, and a big payoff from short sale position, because they believed that the $1.2 trillion dollars of sub prime mortgage assets held by the banks should translate to a substantial operational loss for the banks, because of the credit quality of the borrowers and the reset feature of the loan product which will eventually cause the borrowers to start defaulting. But the banks had already disposed about 80% of the sub prime product through securitization in structured finance, and the risk in those assets was spread out, and distributed all over the world.

The remaining sub prime assets still held by the banks was estimated to be about $300 billion, well within the bank's risk tolerance, even if, all the loans were to default.
The default percentage of all sub prime mortgage at that time was estimated to be about 10%, even though interest rate was higher than it was when the loans were first originated, even

though the housing market was slowing in its normal cycle. The banks were doing ok. The economy was going through a normal slow cycle, before further expansion and continued growth could occur. The situation was quite manageable by the banks.

The generally accepted accounting principle called, historic cost accounting model or book value accounting model made it possible for the banks to own these long term assets that are still performing, and still showing profitability in their quarterly earnings report, instead of a loss, as the mark-to-market accounting model will require them to do.
 The banks were in good shape, still doing well, and their balance sheet looks good.
The situation was quite manageable by the banks.
(until Christopher Cox intervened on behalf of the Hedge Fund short sellers, and changed the rules in the middle of the game by removing the uptick rule, the circuit breakers and the trading curb, making it easier for the Hedge Fund short sellers to enter short positions, bear raid a company and destroy them in a very short order. No pun intended.)

The Hedge Fund short sellers lobbied Christopher Cox to change the rules to change the accounting rules, to facilitate the big take down of the banks for shorting profits, to create a condition in our financial markets akin to the conditions in existence during the 1929 stock market crash.
They lobbied Christopher Cox to change the rules to facilitate their plan, to remove all the safeguard regulations that protected the banks and the financial institutions, and, if in the process, all the other publicly traded companies are affected in sympathy, so be it. (more shorting opportunities and more money for them).

So they got Christopher Cox to remove all the safeguard regulations that protected our financial system and capitalism, such as the uptick rule, the circuit breakers, the trading curb, and to introduce new accounting rules that will directly undermine the banks and devastate their balance sheets. That new accounting rule is called mark-to-market accounting.

All these regulatory changes the Hedge Fund lobby sought was in order to create the conditions similar to 1929, that would bring about the collapse and failure of several banks, and to cause panic share declines and frequent stock market crashes, for the sole purpose of making money, profiting from their short positions, which has now resulted in their looting of America to the approximate sum of 11 trillion dollars.

And there has been loss of lives as a result of their scheme, and crime. At least 5 people were mentioned on CNBC for having committed suicide due to financial losses relating to this crisis. And there are more that died in silence, that no one ever heard about, because they never made the news.

So the Hedge Fund's Chief facilitating tool, Christopher Cox went to work, to execute the plan: Following the script innocently written by the late Milton Freidman. They embarked on creating a series of bad government regulations by changing the rules and removing all the safeguard regulations as follows:

To prevent the repeat of the great crash of 1929, in 1938 a safeguard regulation that governs short sale transactions was put into effect, to prevent stock market crashes due to short sale manipulations, putting downward pressure on stocks and causing panic share declines. That 1938 regulation is called the uptick rule. Christopher Cox removed it in July 2007. Yes Christopher Cox on July 6th 2007 removed the uptick rule, the safeguard regulation that protected capitalism and all the publicly traded companies and their shareholders from criminal short selling and stock sell-off manipulations.

After the crash of 1987, circuit breakers and trading curb was implemented because it is believed that program trading caused the 1987 stock market crash. Christopher Cox removed it.
Oh yes, in November 2nd 2007 Christopher Cox removed the circuit breakers and trading curb that was put in place to

reduce market volatility and massive panic stock sell-offs, in order to allow investors time to think before they act.

Guess who is involved in program trading that crashed the market in 1987, the Hedge Funds short sellers.

Historic cost accounting is a generally accepted accounting principle in which on the balance sheet you show a verifiable amount of how much you paid for an item, then calculate and show the depreciation, and also show the current fair market value of that item.
Oh no, that is not good enough for Christopher Cox and the Hedge Fund short sellers.
On July 1st, Christopher Cox through FASB ended the bank's historic cost model or book value accounting model, and changed the accounting regulation to a mark-to-market accounting.

Christopher Cox has now completed, and executed to script, Milton Friedman's writing on the reason for the Great Depression and the great Stock Market Crash of 1929, which is bad government regulations.
Christopher Cox delivered the bad government regulation aspect of the Hedge Fund's scheme to create conditions similar to the Great Depression and the big crash of 1929.
The only remaining question is did Christopher Cox know the full intentions and true motive of the Hedge Fund lobby, Managed Funds Association, when they were lobbying him? Was he an accomplice or was he just a fool? Was he promised or given any thing in return for betraying America?

Sad but true. Christopher Cox betrayed America, he betrayed capitalism, he betrayed all the foreign countries who believed in America and capitalism; he pulled the rug from under them and destroyed their economy.
He aided the Hedge Fund short sellers to loot $11 trillion dollars from American families, American businesses, American banks, retirement portfolios, 401k accounts, retail investors, mutual funds and pension funds accounts.

Completing a triangle of deceit, incompetence and betrayal; Treasury secretary Henry Paulson and the Chairman of the fed Ben Bernanke did not speak up against Christopher Cox; in a collective effort, they cooperated as a team in crisis with no dissenting view, opinion or testimony: Their silence allowed the errors of Christopher Cox to permanently damage the legacy of President George W. Bush, and single handedly destroyed the Republican Party. And if his mistakes are not corrected, it will also destroy the current administration.

The damage Christopher Cox inflicted on the Republican party cuts very deep, into the party's core principle of fiscal conservatism, that today, it is difficult for Republicans, having been disarmed by Christopher Cox, to criticize the democrats for wasteful stimulus packages, or huge government bail out and socialistic measures in dealing with this economic crisis without getting it thrown right back in their face because it all started in a Republican administration.

The Republican party must acknowledge the sins of Christopher Cox and confess to the American people what had gone wrong and in a bipartisan effort, lead the charge to correct the mistakes of Christopher Cox, by putting forward as an alternative to wasteful stimulus packages and bail outs, the implementation of the 7-point action plan solution that I have written about, proposed several times, and will mention again in a few paragraphs coming up.

Christopher Cox gave us all the bad government regulation that caused this economic crisis. He made into the law, the Hedge Fund short sellers' scam, and legitimized their looting of America.
He promulgated a fraudulent business scheme designed by the Hedge Fund short sellers and their lobbyist to defraud the banking industry and their shareholders and all American common investors and the U.S. treasury in extension. A crime has been cleverly committed.
The Senate and the Congress should look into it. Perhaps enact some new retroactive laws to help bring the looters to justice.

Our market has now crashed and broken, even though the fundamentals of American businesses are resilient, but we are heading into a depression because of the bad SEC regulations weighing down on everything, including investment capital, and investor confidence. The Hedge Fund short sellers' mission has been accomplished, and they have made out like bandits. Oh yes, they are bandits: The Hedge Fund bandits.

They will send you emissaries to advise you on how to better regulate them. Don't listen to them. They are speaking for the enemy. Totally disregard their suggestions. They are working for the looters. They want to avoid detection and culpability. Put them in hand cuffs as soon as you can.

You see how Christopher Cox has systematically dismantled all the safeguard regulations that made capitalism work, one after the other?

The Congress through a new legislation, need to reverse all the bad regulatory decisions made by Christopher Cox, all of them, and not just mark-to-market accounting, because, the reversal of just only mark to market accounting wont work just by itself; the short sellers can still take down any company, whether the company has a good balance sheet or not if the uptick rule is not reinstated to restrict them from bear raiding the company.

All the rules that protects capitalism that Christopher Cox removed, do work together and cohesively, and not in parts, and that is why this economic crisis has been systemic, spreading from one asset to another; the bandits disabled and dismantled all of them: You will have to reinstate all of them.

When the economy was good, and we were busy being Americans, living our blissful lives, the Hedge Fund bandits were busy plotting and scheming, lobbying Christopher Cox to dismantle the safeguards of capitalism.

They have succeeded. They have done a lot of damage; they have destroyed a lot of capital, and capitalism. They have destroyed investor confidence and people are afraid. They have destroyed a lot of people.

We are in a fight.

This is a fight to save America, to save capitalism and protect us from the disaster of socialism which is fast approaching, if Congress and Senate do not act quickly, and act quickly enough and comprehensively to correct the errors of Christopher Cox.

The following 7-point action plan solution has to be implemented to fix this economic crisis. It has to be done immediately and comprehensively, because they are all linked and interwoven.

(1) Reinstate the uptick rule.

Let me break down this uptick rule, so that those who are not stock market investors or active traders will under stand it.

The uptick rule is a regulation that governs short sale transactions.

To short sell a stock, is to sell a stock that you do not own. Yes, selling something that you do not own. How about that?

It is when you initiate a sell transaction on a stock that you do not own, by borrowing the shares from the brokerage, Lets say the stock price is at $100.00 dollars, and you think that it is either over valued at a $100.00 dollars, or that it will go down in price for whatever reason, You sell it first, without owning it at a $100.00 dollars, hoping and betting, that it will go down in value, so that you can then buy it back at a much lower price, lets say $40.00 dollars. So you sell it first at a $100.00 dollars, and you buy it back at $40.00 dollars, and you profit the difference which will be $60.00 dollars.

And the uptick rule says that before you can short sell a stock that someone should buy the stock first, causing the price to tick up before you can short sell.

You see.

If you are watching the stock quote, whenever you buy a stock, or whenever a buy order executes, the green arrow lights up, and points upward, and the stock price ticks up, or goes up. When you have a lot of buy orders, an overwhelming buy orders, the green arrow lights up, pointing upward, and the stock price goes up much higher.

Also

If you are watching the stock quote, whenever you sell a stock, or whenever a sell order executes, a red arrow lights up and points downward and the stock price ticks down, or goes down. When you have a lot of sell orders, an overwhelming sell orders, the red arrow lights up pointing downward, and the stock price goes down much lower.

And.

When you short sell a stock, it has the same effect on the stock price, as though you were doing a normal sell transaction, the red arrows lights up pointing downward as though you previously owned the stock, but you are now selling it, and the stock price ticks down, or the price goes down.

So to prevent stock price manipulation by short sellers overwhelming a stock by putting downward pressure on it, the uptick rule says that before you can short sell a stock, that someone has to buy the stock first. That buy order will cause the price to tick up, then, you can execute your short sell transaction.

So if we get up in the morning and the market is down, and everyone is afraid to buy any stock, then no one can short any stock either. It keeps the stock price stable. Any downward bias on the stock would be real, and would be from the shareholders, the people who previously bought the stock and own it, but are now selling it, and not from short sellers, who do not previously own the stock.

Before a short seller can execute a short sell transaction, someone has to execute a buy order transaction first. No buy orders executed, then, no short sell order is executed. Stock prices remain stable. Downward pressure, and panic selling manipulation caused by short sellers is prevented. The market does not crash, as long as the equity shareholders do not dump their shares in panic.

The requirement for there to be a buyer first, before you can short sell, is what the Hedge Fund short sellers lobbied for, and succeeded in removing. So that, they can manipulate stock prices by putting downward pressure on it, through an overwhelming short selling pressure, triggering a panic selling, and causing the equity shareholders, the real owners of the stock, to dump their shares in a panic, because the stock price is on a free fall, and it could fall to zero with no uptick requirement, and no buyers in sight. They call it a bear raid.

The uptick rule is a requirement for there to be a buyer first, before you can short sell. A buy order must be executed first, causing the stock price to tick up, each and every time, before you can execute a short sell transaction. And that keeps stock prices stable, prevents stock price manipulation and panic selling, and prevents the stock market from crashing. And it worked very well for 72 years.

The uptick rule is the main safeguard rule that protects all the publicly traded companies, their shareholders, mutual fund investors, 401k investors, retirement portfolios, and capitalism. With out this safeguard rule, investor confidence won't be restored and this crisis will not end as we slide into socialism.

Make no mistake about this. Reinstating the uptick rule is the key to recovery from this crisis. With out the uptick rule being reinstated, no other measure will bring a permanent solution to this crisis except socialism. The uptick rule is the key to the success of capitalism. Restore the uptick rule, it will restore investor confidence, restore the bank's balance sheet, reduce price volatility, and allow for capital appreciation, and encourage capital formation. Reinstate the uptick rule.

(2) End mark-to-market accounting immediately and replace it with historical cost or book value accounting. Again this mark-to-market accounting is destructive, it destroys capital and capitalism. It freezes lending; it freezes investing and slows the appetite for risk. It undermines an investor's confidence to invest, knowing that their seed capital will be marked down to a lesser value.

It is anti freedom, and anti capitalism, when someone can not say, here is a receipt for how much I paid for an item, and this is how much I want to sell it for, and I will hold onto it, until I get my price. And I refuse to lower my price because someone else sold a similar item for a much lower price.

It is very socialistic. It is like a government price fixing. For example, It is like a socialist or communist regime telling you to charge 50 cents for a loaf of bread, because that is the going price in the capital city, or that is what every one can afford to pay.
 It is very capital destructive, It destroys capital and capitalism. Get rid of it.

Mark-to-market accounting is procyclical ,meaning that banking business and profit will boom and flourish during good economic times, and during bad economic times you will have bank failures, because of all the bank's long term mortgage assets that will be marked down to a short term market value, resulting in capital losses. This is madness.

The adoption of mark-to-market accounting is a scam, a fraudulent business scheme plotted by the Hedge Fund lobby-Hedge Fund short sellers, to defraud the banking

industry and their shareholders (the real investors) and defraud America in the process, promulgated by Christopher Cox through the FASB and FAS157.
A crime has been committed.

The Hedge Fund short sellers plotted this adoption of mark-to-market accounting because they knew once the banks assets are marked down, the banks will be showing a loss in their balance sheet, and the effect of a continuous loss in business operation on a stock price is a downward bias. If the bank keep marking down assets, and keep loosing money quarter after quarter, their stock prices will keep dropping quarter after quarter, and the short position taken by the Hedge Fund short sellers will keep printing money for them, quarter after quarter until the stock price of the bank goes to zero, or until, the bank goes out of business, which ever comes first.
A crime has been committed.

Whenever the Hedge Fund short sellers hear the phrase "transparency for investors" they start laughing and giggling. They have fooled every one and looted the banks, and the bank's shareholders; they have fooled every one and looted America. Why do they rob the banks? They robbed the bank because that is where the money is at. That legend is still true today.

"Transparency for investors" is the reason Christopher Cox gave for adopting mark-to-market accounting regulation for the banking industry and the financial institutions.
What investors? I ask. Is it the Hedge Fund short sellers or the bank shareholders?
Who are the real investors here? Christopher Cox?

"Transparency for investors" is the reason that the unsuspecting, innocent but gullible proponents of mark-to-market accounting now uses to defend its usefulness and necessity as an accounting regulation. Because it sounds honorable

27

Transparency for investors is now a very amusing code phrase to the Hedge Fund short sellers because it is ironical. It is the phrase that unlocked the bank's vault; the phrase that they used to defraud the bank shareholders, the real investors. They think it is very funny, amusing and ironic.

The Hedge short sellers have robbed us blind, with the aid of Christopher Cox.

The Hedge Fund short sellers are the looters. They are not investors.

Investors are those that bought and own shares in a company with an expectation for a future price increase, and future increase in value.

Hedge Fund short sellers are not investors, they do not want price appreciation or increase in value, they only want, and have an expectation of a future price decline and decrease in value to the extent that it leads to the collapse and destruction of the companies, the better and more profits for them. They are not investors. They are the financial market looters.

End this fraud now. End mark-to-market accounting for the banking industry. No half measures, or modification, or clarification, or compromise. End it completely and immediately. Get rid of it. If you want the banks to become healthy again, remove mark-to-market accounting and replace it with historic cost accounting model. It will restore the bank's balance sheet, restore investor confidence and encourage investments, and allow for capital appreciation, and promote capital formation.

(3) Discontinue and dismantle trading on all the short ETFs, also called the inverse and leveraged ETFs because they circumvent the uptick rule and violate margin requirements.

If you do not dismantle all these short ETFs, short sellers can still short stocks with out an uptick, even if you accomplish item (1) and reinstate the uptick. The Item (3) the short inverse leveraged ETFs were designed by the

Hedge Fund short sellers and their broker dealers to sink their hooks deeper into the market and get around the uptick rule just incase a new administration reinstates the uptick rule. They are formidable and relentless. They are Well dug in, and dug in deep. You have to uproot and eradicate them. To allow the banks to get healthy, restore their balance sheet, restore investor confidence, and allow for capital appreciation and capital formation.

Short ETFs, inverse. Or leveraged ETFs, is a loop hole for shorting stocks without an uptick. You need to close the loop hole, by simultaneously, reinstate the uptick rule, end mark-to-market accounting, and Discontinue and dismantle trading on all the short ETFs, to wrestle control of the stock market and our national economy from the Hedge Fund short sellers - Managed Funds Association, in order to end their control and manipulation of the stock market. And that will, and only that, will restore investor confidence, restore the bank's balance sheet, and allow for capital appreciation, and encourage capital formation.

(4) Reinstate the circuit breakers and the trading curb.

(5) Regulate the Hedge Funds just like you do mutual funds and pension funds.

Stop the Hedge Funds from day trading activities. They are the source of all the great market volatility and every thing bad that happens on Wall Street. They are out of control since Christopher Cox removed the uptick rule and the circuit breakers. Regulate them to be buy and hold investors just like mutual funds and pension funds. Hedge Funds have a bigger impact on the market than mutual funds and pension funds. They control 75% to 90% of trading activities in the market.
They manipulate and collude to determine the direction of the market. They are, a money manufacturing factory, and the commodities that they are processing, are the regular investors, retirement portfolios, 401k investors, mutual fund and pension fund investors.

Without the uptick rule to restrict their shorting activities, the deck is overly stacked in their favor against all investors. Regulate the Hedge Funds. It will restore investor's confidence, reduce price volatility, encourage price stability, allow capital appreciation, and encourage capital formation.

(6) Regulate speculation in crude oil futures by banning margin and leveraging except for the airline industry or any other end user that would actually take delivery of the commodity.

We have seen this over and over. Whenever the economy recovers, they run up the price of crude oil by speculation, and that is inflationary, causing the Federal Reserve to engage in bad monetary policy, fighting inflation and economic growth by raising interest rates. High crude oil price is not good for our economy and national security. It is an indirect tax to the American public, and a source of funds and financing to countries that hate America and capitalism.

(7) Use bail out money to keep people in their homes by reducing their mortgage payments substantially enough to make a difference. Set fixed rate mortgage at 3.5% for all residential home loans including jumbo loans.

No bridge loans or stimulus package will end this crisis. Unless the above mentioned 7-point solution is implemented.

Put back the rules that Christopher Cox removed. And remove the new ones he put in, and watch the biggest rally on Wall Street and global markets unfold, the likes of which we have never seen, and it will mark the end of this economic crisis and the beginning of the recovery because it will restore the bank's balance sheet, attract more investor capital, restores everybody's 401k account, stabilize the financial markets, stabilize the economy, put an end to job losses and lay offs, curb inflation, put an end to high crude oil prices, and restores investor confidence. And American families can invest again and confidently plan their retirement without fear of panic share declines and stock market crashes caused by corruption and manipulation by nefarious Hedge Fund short sellers. Our economic stability and investor confidence will be restored and fully fortified.

Simply put, at a minimum, the Congress need to put every thing back to the way they were in 2006 before Christopher Cox started fixing things that were not broke.

ADDENDUM.

Should there be a Senate hearing on mark-to-market accounting and the uptick rule.
The following chapters and paragraphs are on how I will question the witnesses, If I was a lawmaker, because I have watched, Christopher Cox, Tim Geithner, and Mary Schapiro make untrue statements. They were either being deceitful, or misinformed, or just pretending.
They make these false statements unchallenged, and they just slither their way through their testimony, or confirmation hearings without any challenge or follow up questions..

This is how I will confront them.

SAMPLE QUESTIONS FOR WITNESSES. (MARK-TO-MARKET)

The main thrust of my questioning, for a witness who supports mark-to-market accounting, is to debunk their claim that investors wanted mark-to-market accounting, by checking the veracity of that claim. And also debunk their claim that mark-to-market accounting did not contribute to this economic crisis.

My line of questioning is to show that the witness is either being dishonest or misinformed when the witness says that mark-to-market accounting is to protect investors and promote transparency, or that investors wanted it.

My line of questioning is to show that a witness is either being dishonest or misinformed when the witness says that mark-to-market accounting did no contribute to this economic crisis.

I will use questions and narratives to make my point.

Christopher Cox. Tim Geithner and Mary Schapiro, have all made public statements in support of mark-to-market accounting, and they have all recited the same reasons why it should remain a regulation as follows:

(1) Transparency for investors.
(2) To protect investors and promote transparency.
(3) Investors wanted this rule.

(The real Investors- equity shareholders did not want any accounting rules changed. They do not even know what mark-to-market accounting is until it became a regulation.

The only 2 special interest groups that wanted mark-to-market accounting regulations are the Hedge Fund short sellers, and the Accountants - some in the accounting industry.

The accountants did not like Sarbanes Oxley, (the accounting reform and investor protection act of 2002), because it leaves the accountants open to lawsuits. The adoption of mark-to-market accounting will nullify the impact of Sarbanes Oxley and remove their vulnerability to lawsuit. The Hedge Fund short sellers wanted mark-to-market accounting to loot the banks and the bank shareholders, for short-trading profits.

So, who are the investors that wanted mark-to-market accounting regulation? The Bank shareholders, or The Hedge Fund lobby-Hedge Fund short sellers-the looting bandits?

Since when do investors start making accounting rules? (Only in a town like Washington DC with lobbyist)

If you want to buy a business, and someone wants to sell you a business, but you do not trust their book keeping, what do you do?

Do you go call the SEC and request an accounting regulation change, or do you go and buy from someone else whom you trust their book keeping?

Have the witness give you the names of the so called investors, who wanted the adoption of mark-to-market accounting. Have the witness give you a list of names of the so called investors that actually requested in writing, or complained in writing, about the generally accepted accounting principle being used at the time, called book value accounting, or historic cost accounting model prior to July 1st 2008

Do not let the witness just name a famous public figure that supports mark-to-market. Have them present a written documentation dating back to before July 1st 2008.

We are looking for the so called investors that were there in the beginning that wanted the regulation changed. Those are the plotters and the looters; they are the Hedge Fund short sellers and their emissaries, and lobbyist.

My guess is that, the witness will not even give you one name, because there are no investors. This whole adoption of mark-to-market accounting is a scam. Like I said:
It is a fraudulent business scheme plotted by the Hedge Fund short sellers-Hedge Fund lobby to defraud the banking industry and their shareholders, (the real investors) and defraud America in the process, promulgated by Christopher Cox at the SEC, through the FASB and FAS 157.
A crime has been committed. You have been lied to, and bamboozled.
The U.S. Congress, the Senate, President Bush, and the American public, has been lied to, and bamboozled, in the biggest fraud in human history.

But, should the witness be bold enough to give you any names. I guarantee you, the names will not be that of mutual fund investors, or retirement portfolio investors, or 401k investors, or private investors, or bank shareholders, the equity investors.

Since we are talking about an accounting regulation for the banking industry and financial institutions, the only investors that should really matter, according to their claim of wanting to protect the investors and promote transparency should be the bank shareholders and not Hedge Fund short sellers. Hedge Fund short sellers are not investors.

Investors always want their stock value to appreciate in price and value. Hedge Fund short sellers always want the investor's stocks to decline in price and value, and if possible to zero, or until the company goes out of business.
Hedge Fund short sellers are anti investors.

That is why they laugh and giggle when ever they hear the phrase "transparency for investors" as being the reason for adopting mark-to-market accounting, because they know, they are not investors, because they know, they are anti investors, because they know that they just defrauded the real investors and are getting away with the loot scot-free.
Their primary objective is always to destroy the investors' capital. The primary objective of a short seller is to gain, at the expense of the investor. In the financial market jungle, we call Wall Street; short sellers are the natural enemies of the investors.

And that is why they find it all funny and amusing because it is ironic, that the investors who were supposed to be protected by the SEC were delivered to the anti investor for slaughter, by the same SEC whose mission is to protect the investors.
They let in the wolves in sheep's clothing, into the sheep barn.

You guys should be angry about this fraud, and appoint a special prosecutor to bring these looters to justice. Follow the money. I am receiving emails of individuals making $18 billion dollars, from this crisis in less than one year. Some Hedge Fund short sellers have seen their short position gain more than 600 %, individuals making $15 billion, $8 billion and 3 billions in very short periods of time. Are you kidding me? A crime has been committed. Follow the money, and round them up. This is easy to do. There are money paper trails. Follow the money. Where did all the money go? Follow the money.

(Back to the witnesses)

Should the witness be bold enough to give you names? Call those individuals, whose names were provided as witnesses, and question them under oath.

Find out what qualified them to be investors. What qualified them to want the accounting regulations changed for banks and financial institutions?
Are they bank shareholders?
Do they own stocks in any banking or financial institution for a period of 3 years or more leading up to July 1st 2008?
Did they own stocks in any bank or financial institution in September 2008?
Did they short any bank shares or short any financial institution share prior to July 1st 2008
Did they short any bank shares or short any financial institutions shares in September 2008

MORE QUESTIONS FOR WITNESSES. (MARK-TO-MARKET)

Christopher Cox, Tim Geithner, and Mary Schapiro have all made public statements in defense of Mark-to-market accounting, and they have all recited the same lines as follows:
(1) Mark-to-market did not contribute to this economic crisis

I can't believe that these people can make such a dishonest statement in front of lawmakers and no one questioned their veracity. No follow up questions?

Follow up questions as follows:

What is procyclical?
Is mark-to-market accounting procyclical or countercyclical?
What happens when you pay $50 million dollars for an asset, but you have to mark it down to a short term value of $20 million dollars? Have you not lost $30 million dollars in short term value? Yes or No?

When a company looses money, what is more likely to happen to the share price of that company, does it go up or does it go down?
What happens to a business that looses money continuously, quarter after quarter after quarter?
When a company goes out of business, would the employees loose their jobs?

What type of economic crisis are we having?
What are the symptoms of this economic crisis?
Which of the following do you think is not a symptom of this economic crisis?

(1) Job losses and Unemployment?   (2) lack of lending or credit crunch?
(3) Deteriorating bank balance sheets? (4) Capital destruction?
(5) Lack of appetite for investment risks?
(6) Lack of confidence and unwillingness to invest and unwillingness to lend?
(7) Falling home prices?
(8) Fallen stock prices, depressed 401k portfolios and retirement portfolios?

Which of the above listed symptoms, is not caused by mark-to-market accounting?
(I will repeat the above list).

All of the above listed symptoms of this economic crisis are all caused by mark-to-market accounting. So don't let the witness get away with making dishonest statements such as:

"Mark-to-market contribution to this economic crisis is not a significant factor".
Mark-to-market is a major contributing factor to this economic crisis.
Mark-to-market accounting contributed enormously to this economic crisis as follows:

(1) Job losses and Unemployment.
Several banks that are affected by mark-to-market accounting have closed causing unemployment and job losses

(2) Lack of lending or credit crunch.
Banks are unwilling to lend because they do not want to put their capital at risk for fear of invested capital being marked down in 3 months or so.
Because mark-to-market accounting is procyclical, banks are reluctant to lend in a down cycle.

(3) Devastated bank balance sheets
Affected banks are lining up for bail out and Tarp money.

(4) Capital destruction.
Devastated bank balance sheets with each mark down and loss of investment capital with each mark down.

(5) Lack of appetite for investment risks.
Private capital does not want to loose their money during the next round of mark downs.

(6) Lack of confidence and unwillingness to invest and unwillingness to lend.
Bankers do not want to lend. Borrowers do not want to borrow, for fear of potential mark down.

(7) Falling home prices.
More foreclosure homes flooding the housing market due to unemployment increasing home supply and decreasing demand.

(8) Fallen stock prices, depressed 401k portfolios and retirement port folios.
With each mark down means more losses and no profits. Share prices plummet
Weak financial and banking stocks mean weak economy and weak market. Depletion of equity capital, Stock market will not rally: continued depression in 401k and retirement portfolio.

WITNESS QUESTIONS: UPTICK RULE:

The removal of the uptick rule, circuit breakers and trading curbs are just indefensible.
I have not seen any existing Congressional witness testimony on the uptick rule. But confront the witness similarly to the mark-to-market accounting proponent witnesses.

Question the truthfulness of any reason that the witness gives you for supporting the removal of the uptick rule.
For example:
Whether he consulted with any one before removing the rule? Who lobbied for it?
Did any one do a research report in support of removing the rule?
Did any one write a report analysis in support of removing the rule?
Whomever that did the study in support of removing the uptick rule, do they have a relationship with the Hedge Fund industry, a Hedge Fund manager or company before or after the report was written?
Ask for proof and documentation of studies before and after rule was removed?

Who were the so called investors that wanted the removal of the uptick rule?
Who were the investors that said it was out dated and not necessary any more?

Who were the so called investors that told you that circuit breakers and trading curbs were out dated and no longer necessary?

Have the witnesses name names. Those are the architects that plotted the looting of America.

Were any of the so called investors, involved with Hedge Funds short selling?
Were any of the so called investors a broker dealer that shorts stocks?
Have you done any studies of market volatility since July 6th 2007?
There has been excessively more volatility since the uptick rule was removed. Yes or No?
Does the witness know that we had a more severe market crash than 1929?
Does the witness know that the rule was put in place to prevent a repeat of the 1929 stock market crash?

In conclusion, please remember that the solution to ending this economic crisis, simply put, is to put everything back the way it was in 2006 before Christopher Cox started fixing things that were not broken. Now that you know the truth and the root cause of this economic crisis, you need to inform your colleagues and start putting everything back to how it was in 2006 at a minimum. But for capitalism and our economic system to emerge from this crisis fully restored, stronger and more fortified than before, you must implement all the following action plan solution I mentioned earlier, as follows:

1. Reinstate the uptick rule.
2. End mark-to-market accounting, and replace it with a historical cost accounting model.
3. Discontinue and dismantle trading on the short ETFs because it circumvents the uptick rule and violate reg T margin requirements.
4. Regulate the Hedge Funds just like you do mutual funds and pension funds. Reinstate the circuit breakers and trading curb.

5. Regulate speculation in crude oil futures by banning margin and leveraging except for the airline industries or any other end user that would actually take delivery of the commodity.
6. Use money from the approved $700 Billion rescue bill to address the mortgage and sub prime issues by keeping people in their homes through lower payments on fixed rates loan restructure. For the fixed rate home mortgage, set interest rate at 3.5% for all residential loans including jumbo loans.

When you implement the above listed action plan solution to solve the economic crisis. Or at a minimum,
when you put everything back the way they were before Christopher Cox.
There is still one more thing left to do. Recover the stolen money.

Now that the Hedge Funds short sellers have looted the banks, and the bank shareholder, and has every body's money and stocks are selling way below book value. They are in a very good position to take advantage of a very deeply discounted stock market, very deeply discounted stock prices and other assets, unless you go after them, and recover the stolen money, and put them in jail.
Crime does not pay. Their crime should not go unpunished.
People have died as a result of their scheme, and crime.
You really need to follow the money and round them up and put them in hand cuffs.

You may begin your investigation at the Washington DC office of Managed Fund Association. They lobbied to have the rules changed, and their members benefited most from this economic crisis. Their members have the bank's money and every body else money too. They should be your primary looting suspects pending your conclusive investigation.
The following Hedge Fund short sellers and their lobbyist lobbied Christopher Cox and the SEC: Jim Chanos, Richard Baker, Eric Vincent, John G Gaine, and others, people that work for them, and on their behalf.

Let me know if you want a list of witnesses who could testify in favor of ending mark-to-market accounting and Reinstating the uptick rule.

Feel free to call me for any questions or further discussions.

Thanks.

Sincerely

(So ended my letter to the congress, a version of which I sent to the Honorable Bill Isaac. The following are the results of my investigative research, when the congress did not want to investigate Managed Funds Association)

WIZARDS OF WALL STREET & WASHINGTON LAP DOGS

A CULTURE OF CORRUPTION

THE SCAM

THAT ELECTED BARACK OBAMA

Several months have now passed since I suggested to the Congress and the Senate to follow the money and start their investigation of Managed Funds Association. It appears to me that as soon as I started mentioning names, the names of the perpetrators, there was reluctance in them pursuing this matter any further. But I won't be deterred. I want the truth to get out; I want the bandits exposed; and I want them to be held accountable for their crimes.

Congress does not want to act on this matter so I started my own investigation; I started digging for more information on Managed Fund Association and their activities.
The things I am finding out are just jaw dropping.

If Congress and Senate decide to find the perpetrating looters and follow the money, It will lead them right to the members of Managed Funds Association and their alliances.
If Congress and the Senate investigates Managed Funds Association; with the Investigation beginning at the Washington DC and New York offices of Managed Funds Association, what will they find, a can of worms?

Oh Yes, a can of worms. A can of worms that would reveal a cabal of slithery powerful men, a cabal of slithery campaign contributors and big money fund raisers who plotted to defraud the banking industry and their shareholders and in the process, they defrauded America.
A can of worms that will reveal the scam that resulted in the election of Barack Obama.

A can of worms?

A can of worms that will reveal that the cabal, the plotting looters, calculated that if they could crash the market and crash the national economy to a doomsday scenario, and then strike the electorates with enormous financial crisis, collapsing economy, job losses, home foreclosures, and crisis of confidence, fear and frustration, with no solution in sight, the Electorates would go into the voting booth with fear in their hearts and a change of government in their minds. Thus, the cabal gets the amiable government they wanted, and gets a lot richer in doing so.

So it was.
The electorate was struck with enormous financial crisis, collapsing economy, job losses, and home foreclosures, crisis of confidence, fear and frustration with no solution in sight. And the electorates went into the voting booth with fear in their hearts and a hope for a better tomorrow that only change could bring; hence, the election of Barack Obama.

The electorates have been tricked, scared, frightened and bamboozled. The electorates went into the voting booth with fear in their hearts. It was fear that clouded their minds. It was fear generated through manipulation by a man-manufactured forced collapse of our financial system and national economy. The economic crisis was deliberately engineered for political gain and profit.
They collapsed the economy, crashed the stock market, blamed the incumbent administration and consumer culture; the Republicans took the fall for it. Obama became president. It was a scam. It was a swindle. It was set up.

MFA members the Hedge Fund short sellers set up the Republicans to take the fall for the economic collapse through the Republican Party betrayer in chief, Christopher Cox.

They went to the gullible fool Christopher Cox and said to him, Hey Mr Cox, or shall we call you Mr Deregulator / Republican.

You love deregulation right?

Please deregulate this for us.
We are investors, and this uptick rule is kind of old and irreconcilable with our modern computers, it is not needed any more, can you please suspend it, also while you are at it, please remove the circuit breakers and the trading curbs, these are modern times, improved with electronics and technology, all these old regulation are not needed anymore because of modern technology please get rid of them. Oh and don't forget, this historic cost or book value accounting model that the banks are using are actually not a true and accurate representation of the value of their assets; the banks are lying about the value of their assets. We need them to have transparency in their accounting model; we are investors, we need to be able to trust their book keeping to make investment decisions, the accounting model that they are currently using allows them to lie and play with the numbers, compel them to mark their assets to the current market prices. Impose mark to market accounting regulation on them to keep them honest.

Christopher Cox complied. Either he was paid off big time or he is an incompetent fool unable to differentiate between good necessary regulation that is required to protect property ownership, and bad unnecessary regulations which hampers free market capitalism. He gave them everything they asked for. I suspect they rewarded him for his very important role in their scam. One of his department Chiefs, Stuart Kaswell is now working for Managed Funds Association as an executive vice president; a reward for his role in the scam.

These Hedge Fund short sellers through their lobbying company MFA were lobbying Christopher Cox SEC to remove all the regulations that were put in place to prevent a stock market crash and a repeat of the great depression from occurring. And they were Barack Obama supporters. They asked the SEC to remove the safeguard regulations that protected capitalism; that protected all our publicly traded companies and their share holders; the invested capital assets of millions of Americans and Christopher Cox said yes.

In a capitalist system economy, wealth and method of producing wealth is privately owned, operated and traded for profit; that trading aspect of capitalism is facilitated by credit and financing, where private equity ownership appreciating in value overtime, attracts investment interests and capital, through capital formation.

The people who provide the funds, the people who provide the capital for financing growth must be protected from those who want to steal their capital through crooked means or fraud. And that is the function of the uptick rule, to protect the invested capital, to protect the publicly traded companies and their share holders from the short sellers who can manipulate stock prices, by putting downward pressure on stocks in the absence of the uptick rule and when there are no buyers.

We can not have unbridled capitalism. There is no capitalism unless the capital is protected by law. For capitalism to work, it must operate within the law; within some rules and regulations that protects private property ownership; and that was the function of the uptick rule. It protected the investment capital of the equity shareholders.

Historic cost or book value accounting preserves the value of the asset property and allows the property owner to hold on to their property until they can get the price satisfactory to them. Managed Fund Association lobbied the SEC and FASB to impose mark to market accounting regulation on the banks and financial institution forcing them to mark down their long term assets to a short term market value, devaluating the bank's assets for shorting profits to hasten their collapse.

How is this underhanded malicious scandalous criminal maneuver by the Hedge Fund short sellers possible? It is possible because politicians, policy makers and regulators through special interest lobbyists, indiscriminately take money from whomever is willing to pay for their influence; even from a foreign enemy government if they can get away with it. (Saddam, Qaddafi and the Chinese governments, all had Washington lobbyists. Someone accepted their money).

It is possible because of the power of money, lobbying and corruption. The Washington DC's culture of influence peddling and corruption usurped the power of the people's representative government (by the people for the people) and enthroned the Wizards of Wall Street lobbyists, Managed Funds Association members, the Hedge Fund short sellers as the dominating influence in policymaking and regulatory reforms. Consequently, benefiting just a few instead of the many (masses)   Benefiting the Hedge Fund short sellers and their Washington DC lapdogs, both of whom have been gorging themselves at the expense of the American people, gorging themselves at the expense of the public good.

There was $5.5 billion dollars spent by lobbyist to influence and control banking and financial market regulations through obtaining regulatory changes in favor of their special interest group at the expense of the American public interest and the common investors.

This expenditure of $5.5 billion occurred over a ten-year period. The first depression era safeguard regulation they lobbied for and succeeded in removing was the Glass Steagall Act, removed in 1999 by President Clinton, Bob Rubin, Sandy Weil and Phil Gram. Even though the removal of the Glass Steagall Act did not cause a national economic crisis, it did set the precedence for tinkering and meddling with the depression era banking and financial regulations.

The beneficiaries of the removal of Glass Steagall Act made a lot more money, kicked back a lot more money to the politicians through the proper legal channels called: campaign contributions, political fund raisers, lucrative consulting contracts, hefty speaking fees, appointment to a board of director membership, guaranteed future job offers, employment as a lobbyist, and sometimes out right cash payments and bribery, perpetuating the culture of corruption. The circulation of money flow between lobbyist - special interest groups and politicians continues in perpetuity. Consequently, it resulted in bold aggressive greed for money and power grab agenda by the key players that completely eroded the interest of the American public.

The elected officials do not represent the best interest of their constituents anymore. They do whatever the heck they want

46

to do, meaning, they do whatever the lobbyists want them to do, meaning, they will do whatever the lobbyist will pay them for, with no exception, including selling out their constituents or selling out their country, piece by piece. This includes dismantling the safeguards of capitalism and replacing them with Marxist punitive measures and regulations, piece by piece, and screw the country.

That is exactly how they unthreaded the fabrics that held capitalism together. Now they are at the verge of outright ripping that fabric apart, saying that capitalism never worked and that it is flawed.

This is one of the reasons why I want the truth about what caused this economic crisis to be known, to let the truth be known about those people who had worked to subvert our economic system called capitalism by lobbying and succeeded in removing its underpinnings beginning in July 2007.

I want the truth, to be known about those people who worked to subvert our economic system for financial and political gain. The schemers and plotters who plotted, defrauded the banking industry and their shareholders, and defrauded America in the process, and continue to mislead and defraud America in her confusion, perplexity and fear mired in an economic depression. Those people are whom I am referring to, as the Wizards of Wall Street, and their Washington lap dogs.

On Wall Street, there are two Wall Streets: the good Wall Street, the long only, wealth creating, business building, job creating Wall Street, the investment banks, long only Hedge Funds, and the other Wall Street, the bad Wall Street, the short only, the Hedge Fund short sellers, the liquidity takers, investment capital destroyers, the Hedge Fund short sellers

An example of the good Wall Street would be someone like Warren Buffet, Steve Jobs or Sandy Weil, and many more.

An example of the bad Wall Street would be someone like George Soros, Jim Chanos, John Paulson and many more.

47

For the good Wall Street to make money, prices have to go up, everybody makes money, the companies and their shareholders make money, jobs are safe and secure, the economy grows, and the economy expands. The action of the good Wall Street grows and expands the economy.

For the bad Wall Street to make money, prices have to go down, which means that companies and their investors have to loose money or sometimes the companies may have to be totally destroyed. People have to loose money and loose their jobs. The action of the bad Wall Street, destroys companies, takes away liquidity, destroys investor capital, slows down the economy, ends economic growth and expansion, and destroys the economy.

The good Wall Street, lobbied for and obtained the repeal of Glass Steagall Act in 1999, and that was good for economic growth and expansion, and that was good for America and capitalism.
(Warren Buffet or Steve Job were not involved in lobbying for the repeal of Glass Steagall Act)

Then, entered the bad Wall Street saying, " If the good Wall Street can lobby for and obtain regulatory changes, and make lots of money, why can't the bad Wall Street do the same?"
So the bad Wall Street, the Hedge Fund short sellers, the liquidity takers, the investor destroyers, and capital destroyers set out to lobby for regulatory changes, but not to just make a lot of money, but to set up an oligarchy, and take everybody's money, and create a balance sheet crisis for the whole nation. They want all the money in America, destroying everything on their path, destroying and burying the good Wall Street, even if that means destroying America and capitalism, so be it. And so, they have begun the process. They will establish an oligarchy. And so they have done just that.

So the "bad" Wall Street, the Hedge Fund short sellers, set out to lobby for the removal of the safeguard regulations that protected capitalism and risk taking, the safeguard regulations that protected the good Wall Street, the safeguard regulations that protected all the publicly traded companies and their shareholders, the investors, the business lending, business building, job creating, goods and services, and manufacturing investors. The bad Wall Street, the Hedge Fund short sellers, set out to lobby for the end of free market capitalism and the Washington lap dogs rolled over onto their backs and said yes, yes, and yes for the bribery treats of campaign contributions, political fund raisers, lucrative consulting contracts, hefty speaking fees, appointment to a board of director membership, guaranteed future job offers, guaranteed future employment as a lobbyist, and some times, out right cash payment bribery.

The Hedge Fund short sellers were initially lobbying to prevent a stronger regulation of their industry and seeking a better understanding of their industry from policy makers and regulators, but has since switched to a more aggressive dominant posture, a more aggressive dominant attitude as their influence grew, and they bought the right from the policy makers and the regulators through the proper legal channels of bribery and corruption, they have become the only recognized voice to speak on behalf of all investors and the investment community. As a result, they embarked upon misleading policy makers and regulators, impersonating and usurping the real investors through a disguise of their intentions, deceitful and misrepresentation of their true identity and concealing their ulterior motives. They are truly and completely dirty liars, cunning crafty wizards.

With Christopher Cox as the SEC Chairman, and the Democrats controlling both houses in 2007, their boldness and influence grew and expanded from being the only recognized voice to speak on behalf of all investors to being the voice that writes the regulations for all investors and being the voice that makes demands on the regulators on behalf of all investors. Whatever they asked for, Christopher Cox gave them.

Christopher Cox gave Managed Fund Association, the Hedge Fund short seller's lobbying company everything they asked for and wanted. Starting from July 2007, Christopher Cox systematically dismantled all the safeguard regulations that protected capitalism, and our publicly traded companies and their shareholders, by removing the uptick rule, removing the circuit breakers and trading curbs, and brought back a previously abolished accounting regulation that caused several bank failures in the 1930s era, called mark-to-market accounting to defraud the banking industry and their shareholders at the request of Managed Funds Association.

It took the lobbyist, policy maker and regulators ten years of influence peddling, bribery and corruption to come full circle in dismantling all the 1938 safeguard regulations, and all the 1987 subsequent stock market regulations addressing the impact of computerized program trading. However, the consequential regulations that they removed, with the help of Christopher Cox, which caused the economic crisis are the safeguard regulations that were put in place to protect capitalism, risk taking, our publicly traded companies and their shareholders. These regulations prevented stock price manipulation, panic share price decline, massive stock market volatilities, and stock market crashes.

These consequential safeguard regulations were dismantled and removed in 2007 and 2008; and they were namely, the uptick rule, the circuit breakers, trading curbs, and the introduction of mark-to-market accounting, which resulted in the collapse of several banks, and the economy, punctuated by a very violent stock market crash, thus leading to a depression.

The 1999 removal of the Glass Steagall Act did not cause the economic crisis. The U.S. economy grew and expanded for most of the eight years following the removal of the Glass Steagall Act. The economic crisis was caused by the other depression era regulations removed in 2007 and 2008 as I just mentioned above: Namely, (1), The removal of the uptick rule on July 6th 2007. (2) The removal of the circuit breakers and trading curbs on November 2nd 2007. (3) The introduction of mark-to-market accounting regulation imposed on the banks, and financial institutions on July 1st 2008. That is what caused the economic crisis.

The 1938 regulations and the subsequent 1987 regulations were all put in place to prevent a repeat of the Great Crash of 1929 and another Great Depression.

The 1938 and 1987 regulations served the purpose of preventing panic selling, massive stock market volatilities, stock price manipulation, panic share declines and stock market crashes that could lead to an economic depression.

So as soon as they unhinged and knocked down these safeguard regulations in 2007 and 2008, the market crashed and crashed frequently, the economy collapsed, and the depression set in.

Ten years of tinkering and meddling with banking and financial market regulations. A ten years of gradual erosion of representative government in banking and financial regulatory and policy making bodies, where politicians and regulators peddle their influence on behest, or request from lobbyist of special interest groups for campaign contributions, political fund raisers, lucrative consulting contracts, hefty speaking fees and future job guarantees and sometimes outright cash payment and bribery at the expense of the American public interest, the American consumers and common investors, to the detriment of our nation, national economy, and national security culminated in the abusive boldness for power grab and greed to plot and defraud the banking industry and their shareholder which resulted in the looting of America and the collapse of the national economy, the greatest economic crisis this nation has faced since the Great Depression.

The politically appointed regulators and the publicly elected officials in key policy making roles do not serve the American public interest any more; they are serving the interests of the lobbyist of the special interest groups. However, when it comes to banking and financial market regulators and policy makers, they are not serving the interest of the American people; they are serving the interest of Managed Funds Association members, the Hedge Fund short sellers, at the expense of American public interest and the common investors.

The $5.5 billion dollars investment in lobbying expenses and political contributions (bribing and corruption) has netted the Hedge Fund short sellers about $11 trillion dollars of looting profit, stolen from the banking industry, equity shareholders, 401k employees, common investors and retirement portfolios.

It is common for lobbyist to work both sides of the aisle in Washington DC. In the case of Managed Funds Association, when you are dealing with Hedge Fund short sellers, they are occupationally two-faced, secretive and deceitful, always angling for the most profitable trade or position. These are people that can pretend to be your friend. Let's say you are the Chief Executive Officer of a publicly traded company worth about $5 billion dollars and some of these Hedge Fund short sellers are your friends, they will not hesitate or feel any qualms about secretly short selling your company for profits until you are driven to bankruptcy and destruction. They will then send you a hundred thousand dollar ($100,000.00) birthday gift. What a friend!

They will raid and loot your company for $5 billion dollars and then send you a birthday gift worth $100,000.00 dollars and justify their action by arguing that your company was over valued and they had to discover the true value of your company and provide an investment opportunity for others to buy into your company at a good value, if your company has any redeeming value. However, all their activities in destroying your company are kept secret from you.

Will the politicians have the courage to investigate Managed Funds Association?
Do they want to find the Links between Managed Fund Association members and the Obama administration?
Do they want to find out the true role of Managed Funds Association members in creating this economic crisis, looting

the banking industry and their shareholders, sinking the U.S. economy, scaring and manipulating the electorates into the election of Barack Obama?

Are the politicians and justice department willing to discover the whole cabal of slithery two-faced, lying, deceitful, rich serpents and vultures that scammed the nation, looted America, destroyed capitalism, our national economy and national security and elected the first anti-American president, the first let's-blame-America-first president? Whose goal and strategy is to diminish America, weaken our military by unilateral disarmament and transformational depletion of our national wealth and reserve, through incurring burdensome debt obligation and willful irresponsible wasteful spending and exorbitant heavy taxation of the so called rich and business corporations to permanently stifle our national economic growth, expansion and prosperity?

Are there any grown ups left in the government and justice department?
Are there any American champions left out there?

Managed Fund Association is a very powerful lobbying organization, extremely powerful in Washington these days. They are the lobbying company for the Hedge Fund short sellers. They represent over 1300 members around the world. Their members include those in the Hedge Funds industry, commodities and currency futures, broker dealers, stocks and derivatives exchanges and other companies who provide services to the industry. Such as companies that conduct studies (Empirical Evidence Report and Write Report Analysis) for the SEC and FASB.
Both the SEC and FASB are compromised because they are influenced by Managed Fund Association. Both the SEC and FASB are influenced, to accept, adopt and utilize such a report from one of the companies that are strategic partners of Managed Funds Association.
Managed Funds Association has it all sown up, all angles covered and secure. They are very thorough in covering all bases.

The members of Managed Funds Association manage over $2 trillions in assets. They are relentless in lobbying all the policy makers and regulators in Washington to get them to shape regulations to benefit them at the expense of the common investors, equity shareholders, mutual funds and 401k investors and retirement portfolios. Yes, Managed Fund Association is relentless in lobbying and influencing the regulators and policy makers in Washington to shape regulations to benefit them at the expense of the American public interest, national economic interest, and our national security interest. They do not care about the country. They have established an oligarchy. They want the money, the control, and the power that money brings. They want the power of the King maker. They are the King makers. Christopher Cox, a Republican, made it all possible for them to assume that role. How stupid can he be? He provided the cover for the slithering snakes to strike. He sold out the good wall street to the bad wall street. He made it possible for the bad Wall Street to take over the stock market, take over and control our national economy, take over and control our political system. The bad wall street primed the stock market for manipulation for political gain and profit; they collapsed the economy, crashed the stock market to get Barack Obama elected. Any asset class that is traded in the NYSE, CME, or EUREX is susceptible to manipulation by the members of MFA and their strategic partners; the bad wall street.

For the bad Wall Street to make money, prices have to go down, companies and investors have to loose money, and some times the companies will be completely destroyed, people have to loose money and loose their jobs. The action of the bad Wall Street destroys companies, takes away liquidity, destroys investor capital, slows down the economy, ends economic growth and expansion and destroys the economy. The bad Wall Street are the Hedge Fund short sellers. The Hedge Fund short sellers are represented by Managed Funds Association, a lobbying trade organization for the Hedge Fund short sellers. The bad Wall Street, Managed Funds Association members, the Hedge Fund short sellers are controlling out markets, our national economy, and the Obama administration. The bad Wall Street-the Hedge Fund short sellers are now running the country. They are writing all our banking and financial market regulations and policies. The manipulators, the wizards of Wall Street, the oligarchy are all members of Managed Funds Association.

Managed Funds Association misrepresent themselves as investors, usurping the real investors, the equity shareholders, from the protection of the SEC, whose mission is to protect the real investors as well as maintain fair orderly and efficient market.

Managed Funds Association controls the regulators and policy makers through legal bribery, campaign contributions, political fundraisers, lucrative contract awards, hefty speaking fees, job safety award, and multi million dollar donations.

They mislead the regulators and policy makers by telling them that they are investors without disclosing that they are net short sellers, liquidity takers, and capital destroyers. Even though some of them, sometimes, they can establish a smoke screen long only fund portfolio, their main active trading engagement is in short selling, and they can exit the long fund position at any time and go short on the same company, consuming the company, until it is destroyed.

You will not let a baby eating monster baby-sit your children even if they can be tame 50% of the time. What about the other fifty percent, when it turns around and consumes your children? That is exactly what we have with the regulators and policy makers cooperating with the Hedge Fund short sellers and refusing to regulate them, and continue to shape regulations in their favor against the common investors, contrary to the role and mission of the SEC which is to protect the common investor.

You do not let the fox guard the hen house.

Managed Funds Association and their alliances have been misleading policy makers and regulators for a decade but had practically taken over writing all financial regulatory rules since Christopher Cox was appointed to the SEC in 2006. And they have been very successful in doing so. Their relationship with policy makers and regulators is deep and strong. They work both sides of the aisle. They will recruit Republicans as lobbyists to go after Republican policy makers and regulators, and recruit democrats as lobbyists to go after democratic policy makers or regulators.

Managed Funds Association was founded in 1991 and have been lobbying since then, but starting from 2006 their engagement with policy makers and regulators became more intense, more hands on, more misleading, with more intensity, they started writing the law on all financial regulatory issues in the Senate and house committees and other government regulatory bodies like the SEC, FASB, etc. All the elected or appointed officials had to do was to adopt the proposal from Managed Funds Association and their alliances and make it the law. Talk about outsourcing government regulations. Talk about Washington lap dogs. Talk about these Washington lapdogs outsourcing government policy and regulations to their masters, the Wizards of Wall Street. Talk about corruption in high places.

All our banking and financial markets regulations are being outsource to Managed Funds Association members. All our banking and financial market regulations are being outsource to Hedge Fund short sellers. Can you believe this outrageous abomination?
The policy makers and regulators adopt the recommendations of the Hedge Fund short sellers and turn it into the law. The policy makers and regulators promulgate the recommendations of Managed Funds Association members and their alliances (strategic partners) into the law.

Their influence is far reaching and extensive. Their influence is far reaching and extends into the White House advisory committee. They are influential in political appointments (with or) without the administration being clued in.
They are everywhere, globally positioned to manipulate and exert influence from abroad, manufacturing the appearance of a consensus through cooperative alliances and strategic partnerships.

CABAL OF SLITHERY RICH

So who is the brain behind the agenda of Managed Funds Association? Who is calling the shots? Who are the strategist, schemers and plotters responsible for directing the biggest scam in human history?

The strategy and agenda of Managed Funds Association is set and directed by their founders' council, and their sustaining members, all are major leading Hedge Fund short sellers. Notable names among them are these leading Hedge Fund managers and short sellers, John Paulson, Jim Chanos, George Soros, Kenneth Griffin, David Shaw, James Simon, Philip Falcone, Paul Tudor Jones, Alec Litowitz and others. Implementing the founders' council agenda are their Washington intermediaries, their lobbyists, Richard Baker, Eric Vincent, John G. Gaine and others. These are the people at the helm of subverting our economic and financial market systems for their personal financial gain and political ambitions They are the betrayers of America and capitalism.
These are the men behind the curtain, (like in the movie, Wizard of Oz, these are the men behind the curtain,) the men behind the scam, the manipulators, the wizards of Wall Street. They were Barack Obama supporters. They were big democratic fund raisers and campaign contributors. They were big Democratic Party donors. They were all Hedge Fund short sellers, all members of Managed Funds Association.
They deliberately engineered the economic collapse, the stock market crash for political gain and profit.
Their dirty malicious scandalous criminal maneuvers resulted in the collapse of the economy, the lending freeze, the stock market crash, and their looting of America in excess of $11 trillion dollars in the biggest financial scam and fraud in human history; as they visited financial violence on the American people to get Barack Obama elected; And they visited financial violence on the America people to destroy capitalism, and destroy our capitalist system free market economy, and replace it with Marxist socialist system

economy. They installed themselves as the powers that be, the oligarchies at the helm of what will become the shadow government within the Obama government administration.

They are well educated and they do a great deal of research before taking a short position. And, they have read Milton Friedman's book, *A Monetary History of the United States*. They knew the reason why the market crashed in 1929.They knew the reason why several banks failed in 1929.
They lobbied Christopher Cox to remove all the safeguard rules that were put in place to prevent a similar market crash from occurring. They lobbied Christopher Cox to change the accounting regulation to create conditions akin to 1929 that triggered several bank failures. Christopher Cox said, yes, yes, and yes. Our free and fair market is no more. The system is now broken. The market is now broken.
They are Hedge Fund short sellers. They relish stock market crashes. They love the market to crash. They crashed the market for political gain and profits.

They wanted to crash the market for shorting profits on their bets against the banks that were exposed to sub prime mortgages. They wanted to crash the market for political gain, to discredit the incumbent administration to the benefit of their candidate, Barack Obama.
The Hedge Fund short sellers were Obama supporters.
They threw their support and money behind Barack Obama.

They wanted a crisis of confidence, they created a crisis of confidence and they created the economic crisis. They removed all the safeguard regulations that protected the banks and all the publicly traded companies; they bear raided all the banks and all the publicly traded companies and looted everybody's money. The economy collapsed, people were angry; people were afraid; and they blamed the incumbent administration, rejected the incumbent party and voted for change. Barack Obama became president. The Hedge Fund short sellers made a whole lot of money. And George Soros got his man elected. And George Soros got his revenge, and that was the scam that elected Barack Obama.

George Soros is the mastermind; the man who self proclaimed that he thrives in chaos. He wanted an economic crisis for political gain and profit. He created a crisis of confidence that would ensure his candidate, Barack Obama, was elected president of the United States. He is the money behind Barack Obama.

In a George Soros meeting with democratic strategist, he discussed ways to defeat George Bush, during the 2004 presidential election. They discussed a recent study conducted by Robert Rubin, the former Clinton White House Secretary of Treasury. The study was on the theory of budget deficit, economic confidence, and financial crisis.
In this study, Robert Rubin argues that the Bush tax cuts, ballooning deficit and rising debt could erode public confidence in the U.S. economy that could trigger a crisis of confidence in the market, costing investors huge financial losses. He concluded that it would be a big re-election problem for George W. Bush if that were to occur.

If there was a crisis of confidence in the market, costing investors huge financial losses, Bush would have lost the re-election. The credit for this insightful thought was attributed to Robert Rubin.

The democrats used this study to start attacking the Bush tax cuts and started talking down the economy, albeit to no avail.

George Soros, for his part, was quoted as believing that "one can influence a market by making negative comments against the market and betting against it, even though it could be only temporarily successful. But if one can force the market down, it will have an effect in the real world. If it happens and persists for a few days leading into the day to cast ballots, people might go into the voting booth with fear in their hearts."

And that was exactly the psychological condition of the voters on Election Day, November 4th 2008 that George Soros was able to create through market manipulation that resulted in mass job losses among the voters. The master-minded market manipulation resulted in bankruptcies, foreclosures, unemployment, anger, fear and hopelessness among the voters. This is the very psychological condition of the voters on November 4th 2008 that got his candidate elected while he made billions from the crisis.

George Soros made billions of dollars from the chaos he created, billions of dollars for the self-proclaimed Master of Chaos. It happened just like he said it would. Market was forced down; it had an effect in the real world, businesses collapsed, people were being laid off, foreclosures and bankruptcy persisted, fortune and wealth was lost with frequent market crashes, it happened and continued happening. It happened and persisted for a few days leading into the day to cast ballots. People went into the voting booth with fear in their hearts.

Following the Robert Rubin study and insight I mentioned above, there were concerns then about George Soros panicking the stock market in November 2004 in his zeal to defeat George W. Bush. Articles were written about it. People talked about it. Some in the media talked about the possibility, and the experts concluded that it would not be possible for George Soros to manipulate the market because of panic prevention measures embedded in our capitalist system of economy and financial markets. There were panic prevention measures and safeguards regulations embedded in the fabric of capitalism.

The conclusion by analysis was that the existing regulations put in place to prevent stock price manipulations, panic share declines and massive stock market volatility, like the uptick rule, circuit breakers and trading curbs, made it impossible for someone to manipulate or panic the market. For George Soros to successfully manipulate or panic the market, certain conditions must exist as described below:

(1) George Soros' argument and reason for talking down the market and betting against the market

must be right, valid, and justified, that other traders would be compelled to join him without invitation to equally bet against the market (for shorting profits).

(2) There must be in existence, program trading and computerized trading (without circuit breakers) that would allow other market participants to follow his cue by getting on the same side of the trade as him, that is the short side, and slamming the market down by causing massive volatility on the down side, cutting through stops and support levels.

(3) The existing protection against panic selling must be removed.

George Soros knew this. He knew the concerns of the Bush Administration. He knew about what people were saying about him. He has manipulated markets before. He knows about the obstacles. Those obstacles have to be removed. The condition has to be right.

The non existence of the above three mentioned conditions and the existence of the safeguard regulations, made it impossible for anyone to manipulate or panic the market. George Soros was not able to manipulate the United States stock market in 2004.

George W. Bush won re-election in 2004.

George Soros and other rich democrats, lamenting their defeat at the polls, set out to reorganize their quest for the White House from the grass roots up: Led by Soros, they formed an alliance with the trade unions. They established democratic institutions and think tank organizations such as the Center for American Progress and the Democracy Alliance partnership. Led by Soros' radical agenda, whose objective is to transform America from a capitalist, constitutional republic to socialism; they will begin to transform politics at the state and local levels and dominate key battleground states by sponsoring and making grants to liberal organizations in the media, liberal organizations in the ideas department as well as liberal organizations in leadership and civic engagement. Hence, George Soros and Democracy Alliance partners poured money into groups like Acorn, Move on.org, etc. Soros gained the cooperation between the alliances and MFA.

George Soros, through Managed Funds Association and their alliances, the Hedge Fund short sellers went to the SEC to obtain the regulatory changes they needed, to remove the protection against stock market panic selling.

With the influence of Managed Funds Association at the SEC, the   board members (corrupt deregulators) at the SEC and members of Managed Funds Association with Republican connections forced out the then SEC Chairman William Donaldson for wanting to regulate the Hedge Fund industry. Entered Christopher Cox who gave them everything they wanted.

So what is it, that they wanted, they, meaning George Soros and Managed Funds Association members, the Hedge Fund short sellers? What is it that they wanted that Christopher Cox gave them?

They wanted the conditions necessary as described above, to exist for one to be able to manipulate the market. They wanted conditions similar to the 1929 era which caused the great market crash of 1929 and the Great Depression. They wanted to remove all the regulations that were put in place in 1938 to prevent stock market manipulation and prevent a repeat of the 1929 stock market crash and Great Depression. They wanted all those 1938 safeguard regulations removed.

They wanted the regulation that was put in place to prevent stock price manipulation that causes panic share declines removed. They also wanted to remove the regulations put in place to prevent massive stock market volatility to be removed. They wanted to unleash the machines, the computers to cause maximum damage, volatility and panic. They wanted the circuit breakers and trading curbs removed.

They wanted the ability to control and manipulate the market at will.

Christopher Cox delivered big time for them. He handed the control of the stock market to them. He gave them everything they needed to manipulate the market, and so they did. The Managed Funds Association members, the Hedge Fund short sellers and their alliances manipulated the market.

The first regulation to go was the uptick rule, the short sale regulation, which prevents stock price manipulation that causes panic share decline. The uptick rule was the regulation that protected risk taking. It was the regulation that protected investors and all the publicly traded companies. They removed it.

The second regulations to go were the circuit breakers and trading curbs that had been put in place to prevent massive stock price volatilities. This regulation was to prevent massive violent volatilities, to reduce panic, and to give traders time to think before they acted. They removed it.

The third regulatory change they obtained was the introduction of mark-to-market accounting, imposed it on the banks by the SEC and FASB at the request of Managed Funds Association and their alliances, the Hedge Fund short sellers. This was a regulation that was abolished by President Roosevelt in 1938 for having caused several bank failures which led to the great crash of 1929 and the Great Depression.

They lobbied to have all safeguard regulations removed and Christopher Cox said yes, yes and yes.
They obtained the regulations George Soros needed to help him pre-determine the outcome of the next presidential election. Christopher Cox obliged them.

Hence, when the plot was perfectly executed, our market started crashing every day, leading into Election Day, and resulted in the election of Barack Obama. As you all may remember, after the Republican Convention, John McCain was leading in the polls until the market started crashing every day.

Everyone knows that the economic crisis caused a lack of confidence, fear and distrust of the incumbent administration among the voting public, especially when there was no credible explanation of what caused the economic crisis and stock market crashes coming from the incumbent administration (The Bush Administration) or the opposition, (the democrats). As a matter of fact, no credible explanation was coming from the experts or the economist either. There was no credible solution in sight.

People were afraid. And their conclusion was: they just cannot trust another four years to the incumbent party, Bush-like McCain administration. They wanted change. Change to what? They did not know. They just wanted change. Anything would be better than what they had; they hoped, hence, the election of Barack Obama.

It happened exactly as George Soros theorized.

The conditions non-existent in the 2004 presidential election that made market manipulation and panic selling impossible, became existent in the 2008 presidential election and it made market manipulation and panic selling possible. Because Managed Funds Association, where George Soros is a sustaining member and a founders' council member (with the distinct responsibility of strategic planning, setting and directing the agenda of the organization), successfully lobbied the SEC to remove all the safeguard regulations that prevented stock market manipulation and panic selling.

George Soros' argument for talking down the market and betting against the market was valid and justified, so it appeared. They were wrong about the banks, the housing market, and sub-prime mortgages. They were loosing money until they went and removed all the above mentioned safeguard regulations, and turned their loosing positions into profitable trades, as the housing market, banks, and sub-

prime mortgages along with the stock market and U.S. economy came crumbling down. People lost their fortunes and some lost their lives as a result of loosing their fortune, while the Hedge Fund short sellers made a fortune looting America, looting the banking industry and their shareholders.
George Soros got his man elected and made money doing so.

In the middle of the depression they created, George Soros summed up his experience of the economic crisis that got Barack Obama elected with these following words, "Life is generated at the edge of chaos, so I specialize in this edge of chaos, I am having a good crisis and it is, in a way, the culminating point of my life's work, It's been stimulating." If this is not a confession or an admission of complicity, then I do not know what is.

The strategy and agenda of Managed Funds Association is set and directed by their founders' council and their sustaining members. Notable names among them are John Paulson, Jim Chanos, George Soros, Kenneth Griffin, David Shaw, James Simon, Philip Falcone, Paul Tudor Jones, Alec Litowitz etc. Implementing their agenda are lobbyists Richard Baker, Eric Vincent, John G Gaine and others.
They had to destroy Capitalism to elect Barack Obama President. They had to destroy America to elect Barack Obama; and that is just the beginning, the first step in their quest to diminish America's influence around the world, which is; destroy capitalism and impose socialism – the engineering of the collapse of the greatest nation on earth - The United States of America. The enemies within are members of Managed Funds Association the Hedge Fund short sellers.

Managed Funds Association members engineered the economic collapse, crashed the stock market and looted every portfolio that had exposure to the stock market, and they have been given a seat at the table in the white house. They were Barack Obama supporters. They engineered the economic collapse to get him elected. They had to destroy our country and visited financial violence on the American people to get him elected.

Enough with Obama saying he inherited the economic crisis from George w Bush. The economic crisis was deliberately created for him so that he can become president. The Hedge Fund short sellers who were supporting him created the economic crisis to get him elected. They collapsed the economy, crashed the stock market, looted every portfolio that had exposure to the stock market, and they blamed George Bush, Republicans took the fall for it. Obama became president. This is the biggest scam and fraud in human history. It is a scandal

American people need to know the truth.

Enough with the Democratic Party strategists, pundits and talking heads blaming George w Bush and the Republican party for deregulation and the economic crisis.

It was democratic party donors, big democratic party fundraisers, all Hedge Fund short sellers, members of Managed Funds Association that lobbied the SEC to remove all the safeguard regulations that were put in place to prevent the stock market from crashing; the safeguard regulations that protected risk taking, investment capital and property ownership; the underpinnings of capitalism that protected all the publicly traded companies and their shareholders. They lobbied the SEC to have them removed and imposed mark to market accounting on the banks and financial institutions. They removed the uptick rule, the trading curbs and circuit breakers. They primed the market for a crash. They primed the market for manipulation by making it possible for them, the Hedge Fund short sellers to put downward pressure on stocks causing panic share declines, causing panic selling without any circuit breakers. They recreated the conditions similar to the 1929 era which caused the great crash of 1929 and the great depression. They engineered the economic collapse, crashed the stock market so that Obama can become President. They have been rewarded financially and politically. They have been given a seat at the table in the white house. Their point man and representatives are in the Obama administration's inner most circles. They are in his cabinet.

CONSOLIDATION OF POWER

Managed Funds Association moved to consolidate their power. They sent John Podesta, who is working for George Soros, to lead the Obama administration transition team and that is how they were influential in appointments of key cabinet positions and key appointments relating to banking and financial markets as well as other areas they deem strategically important to them, hence, the appointment of Larry Summers, Tim Geithner, and Mary Schapiro to mention a few.

Managed Funds Association controls the SEC and FASB Their point man at the SEC is Mary Schapiro.

Mary Schapiro maintains and keeps safe all regulatory advantages Managed Funds Association members had gained under Christopher Cox. Nothing is going to change. They are in control.
No matter how many hundreds of thousands or millions of investors requesting the SEC, through a written petition, asking Mary Schapiro, to please reinstate the uptick rule, and end mark-to-market accounting, and reinstate the circuit breakers and the trading curb, nothing is going to change. The few will dominate the many. The few will participate in dark pools, flash orders and front-running transactions to disadvantage the many. The oligarchy is in control.

Even if Congress joins the chorus, requesting the reinstatement of the uptick rule, removal of mark-to-market accounting, or reinstatement of the circuit breakers and trading curbs, the SEC Chairman Mary Schapiro will not do a thing. She will find ways to delay taking action because the oligarchy, MFA, the Hedge Fund short sellers, wizards of Wall Street; the manipulators, do not want her to take any action.

The manipulators will decide when the stock market will run up for no justifiable fundamental reason, and drag other market players to participate or risk being left behind and under perform the indexes. They can do this with the money they looted and convince the administration to chill out, that everything is under control. They will make the first move and reinvest in America, buy the same very companies that they drove their value down, buy them at a fraction of their value, like on a 90% discount, ten cents on a dollar kind of a deal. As they keep buying and the stock market rises, other market players and the public will join the rally, creating the impression that a recovery is on the way. Therefore, the administration and Congress will chill out; no more pressuring their lap dogs, like the ones at the SEC and FASB, to act. The hopeful American public will think that a recovery is on the way, while nothing fundamentally has changed in the economy; everyone is still suffering from the balance sheet crisis the looters, the now oligarchies handed to them in the scam of the century. No meaningful regulatory changes to correct the errors of Christopher Cox will take place; they can crash or rally the market at will: This fact entrenches the looters, the manipulators, members of Managed Funds Association; the Hedge Fund short sellers as the controllers of our financial markets, national economy, national security, government policies and all future major elections and presidential elections. Their man will always win, which means the end of freedom in America as we knew it. The dirty hands of Managed Funds Association members must be exposed. Their power and influence must be exposed and stopped.

There will be no economic recovery until we wrestle the control of our financial markets, our economy, and our government from their greedy bear paws.
The fragile recovery and the recent stock market rally which began on march 9th 2009 was a result of the announcement of the mark to market accounting subcommittee hearing scheduled for march 12th 2009 and the subsequent modification of mark to market accounting on April 2nd 2009 when FASB relaxed the rules, The looters, the Hedge Fund short sellers who stole everybody's money made the first move; they started buying , investing in America with the stolen money, market kept moving higher and they dragged all their financially wounded victims, the mutual funds and individual investors back into the market who were afraid of

being left behind and missing the rally, and since then, the market has continued climbing and never looked back sustained by a very accommodating federal reserve monetary policy; and the banks are healthier as a result of the modification of mark to market accounting. But this minor success achieved in my efforts along with others, with the help of congress, house financial services sub committee to fix what is ailing the economy is in danger of being reversed. Since Managed Funds Association members, the Hedge Fund short sellers got away with the scam of defrauding the banking industry and their shareholders and looting America in the process without any punishment, they want to come back for more. They now want to expand the mark to market accounting rules again. FASB recently announced they will hold a hearing to consider expanding mark to market accounting. This time it should not be a question of how the rule should be applied, but when the rule should be applied. The manipulators now want a permanent choke hold on our banks and financial institutions. They want to manipulate the market and the U.S. economy at will. Our free market capitalism is almost extinct. Managed funds association, the Hedge Funds short sellers needs to be reigned in. They are ruining the country looting the country, and destroying capitalism. They are the source of everything bad on Wall Street, the dominating influence in all financial policy and regulatory matters, with ties to the Administration.

Managed Funds Association has direct access to all the so called independent regulatory bodies like FASB, the SEC, and the Federal Reserve. (They want the Federal Reserve to loose its independence. They want a super regulator who will be answering to them). And of course, they have unrestrained access to the Senate, house financial services and banking committees. They control Washington, our stock market and our national economy by manipulation, bribery and corruption, and have exported their franchise to Europe, for European markets domination, and manipulation.
Managed Funds Association has direct access to President Barack Obama through John Podesta, Larry Summers, Tim Geithner and Mary Schapiro.

Managed Funds Association, encourages its members to contribute both financially and through personal contact and influence to further the organization's agenda.

With members contributing to their political Pac fund the sum of $5000 for each person, $10,000 per couple, and up to $40,000 a year per member, they have a potential campaign contribution war chest of $240 million dollars to $960 million dollars every four years for a presidential election, and that was the Obama juggernaut that we saw during the presidential campaign of 2008.

The Obama money machine we saw during the campaign did not come from $20 dollar contributions from the general public or through the Internet, contrary to what the liberal media wants you to believe. The monies came from Managed Funds Association members bundling money for Barack Obama and passing some of it through the Internet.

Like I said, an investigation of Managed Funds Association members will reveal a dirty can of worms, including campaign finance law violations. But who is going to investigate them, the democratic Congress?

Managed Funds Association members have a potential range of raising $60 million to $240 million dollars a year to spare for political campaign contribution and for mid term elections. This does not include the money key members spend to support their political courses like George Soros did in his campaign against George W. Bush in 2004 in which he spent over $100 million or the $500,000.00 Jim Chanos gave to the Obama campaign.

The regular members of Managed Funds Association know exactly what is going on. They do receive updates informing them of any regulatory changes achieved by their lobbying company. They know how the cows get slaughtered to benefit their organization and its members. Literally, they labor everyday to slaughter the bulls to feed the bears. They owned the stock market under Christopher Cox as Chairman of the

SEC. Now they own the stock market under Mary Schapiro as the SEC Chairman.

The reinstatement of the uptick rule Mary Schapiro told Barney Frank and Chris Dodd in March 2009, that she will impose within 30 days, is going to take her eight months to implement, if ever she does any thing about it at all. She has been floating around a watered down version of that rule. She just does not want to reinstate the rules because Managed Funds Association members, the Hedge Fund short sellers do no want her to reinstate the rules. They do not want to reinstate the original uptick rule; they want to be able to manipulate stock prices at will, without any restrictions.

Managed Funds Association along with other financial industry lobbyists, spent over $5.5 billion dollars lobbying to change government regulations that resulted in and culminated in their looting of America for approximately $11 trillion dollars, by creating an economic crisis, the ultimate disastrous catastrophic financial crisis.

They thrive and prosper by hiring influential people, and each member has to always be pushing the agenda that will benefit the organizations. They are ruthless in their recruiting method and talent search.

If Managed Funds Association perceives someone to be influential, to be an important personality, or an important adversary, or a potential adversary, or had an important position in government, they will snag the person in to work for them.
Managed Funds Association members and their alliances are the masters of corruption, contaminating, compromising and manipulating the influential talent pool. They have now even gone after our national economist, Alan Greenspan, a voice that could be trusted, a voice that could speak up against them. Today Alan Greenspan works for them through John Paulson. John Paulson is a member of the Managed Funds Association and recently retained the consulting services of Alan Greenspan.

TRUTH CONFESSION
THE GUILTY ARE AFRAID

I will talk about John Paulson briefly.

John Paulson is a Hedge Fund manager, a member of Managed Funds Association. In 2006, in the midst of sub prime and option arm lending, John Paulson and several other Hedge Fund short sellers, all members of Managed Funds Association, were shorting the housing market, they were shorting the banks, the lenders, financial institutions with exposure to option arm lending, and the sub prime market, calculating that there would be a huge number of defaults due to the credit quality of the sub prime borrowers and the resetting feature of the loans they took. And that the financial institutions would under perform and loose investment capital due to non performing sub prime mortgage assets. But they were wrong.

As the lenders, bank and financial institutions were generating these mortgages, they were selling them immediately, and they were spreading the risk around the world, through pools of investment assets securitized in structured finance. The only remaining mortgage assets in the banks' portfolios were well within their risk management tolerance.

The banks were doing good; the housing market was stable. The Hedge Fund short sellers were wrong about the housing market and the financial institutions. At the end of the quarter, when the banks and financial institutions reported their earnings, they were making profits; their balance sheet still looked good. The Hedge Fund short sellers who normally do a great deal of research and analysis did not like the way the bankers and financial institutions were accounting for their mortgaged assets. They did not like the generally accepted accounting principle the bankers, lenders and financial institutions were using.

The Hedge Fund short sellers who were betting against the banks and the housing market were loosing money.
John Paulson was one the Hedge Fund short sellers betting against the housing market and the financial institutions.
John Paulson in 2006 was unsuccessful in betting against the sub prime market, betting on a down turn in housing. Housing remained stable, the banks were doing well. John Paulson was loosing money.

Going into 2007, housing remained stable; the banks were still doing well. The Hedge Fund short sellers were loosing money betting against the banks and housing market. John Paulson was loosing money betting against the banks and housing market until they were successful in removing the uptick rule, the circuit breakers and the trading curb and market volatility increased, banking stocks and financial stocks started coming down.

Their theory was working, everything was falling apart, so they went for the jugular; they wanted to drive down the nail into the coffins of the banks and financial institutions. They wanted the accounting regulation changed to disadvantage the banks. They wanted to bring back an accounting regulation that was abolished in 1938 by President Roosevelt for having caused several bank failures. That accounting regulation was called mark-to-market accounting.

John Paulson met with former SEC chairman Harvey Pitt. John Paulson hired Harvey Pitt. According to John Paulson, he said he hired Harvey Pitt to spread the word about Bear Stearns trying to manipulate the mortgage market by proposing to the regulatory body to permit a rewrite and restructure of mortgage loans. And to that I said OK. Question: Spread the news about bear Stearns trying to manipulate the market to whom?

I will say that John Paulson hired Harvey Pitt, a former SEC Chairman, to help him lobby his former colleagues at the

SEC and FASB to change the accounting regulation to mark-to-market-accounting.

John Paulson also had a lunch meeting with George Soros to discuss methods of shorting the housing market successfully. What were the details of John Paulson meeting with George Soros? Was it an update or progress report or an exchange of ideas on shorting strategies? Was it a complete discussion of the scheme to defraud the banking industry and their shareholders, by market manipulation and causing panic share declines and creating an economic crisis, and creating a crisis of confidence to influence the upcoming presidential election? Did they discuss the size of the pot resulting from defrauding the banking industry and looting America?

John Paulson said the pot was as much as $10 trillion dollars and when you multiply Hedge Fund assets in the range of $1.5 to $2 trillion dollars by 600%, the percentage increase in portfolios that were shorting the housing market and financial institutions; you will get a range of $9 to $12 trillion dollars, and that is pretty close to the $11 trillion dollars they stole from innocent law abiding Americans.

Did they discuss reducing and minimizing their publicized earnings from the scam so as not to engender public anger, because the portfolios that shorted the housing market, and shorted sub prime mortgage and held through the crisis were up by more than 600%?

Let's take for instance, Jeff Greene, a California real estate mogul who betted against sub prime mortgage. He saw his portfolio increase more than 600%; some articles says that his portfolio increased 1400% in 18 months; compare that to the type of meager percentage returns attributed to John Paulson and George Soros, something doesn't add up, considering that both men shorted sub prime, housing market, banking and financial institutions earlier than Jeff Greene. They were there in the beginning. They were the architects of the scam.

Jeff Greene was one of the deep pocket clients that John Paulson would mine for funds. In this instance Paulson met with Jeff Greene and pitched a new fund he wanted to open so that Jeff Green could invest in the fund. Instead of Jeff Greene investing his funds with John Paulson, he took the idea and established his own virtual Hedge Fund, a one man Hedge Fund, and copied the strategy Paulson pitched to him. Jeff Greene is not part of the cabal, or a wizard of Wall Street, he was just an investor with a Hedge Fund short seller connection. He invested in sub prime and benefited from the scam perpetrated by Managed Funds Association members, the Hedge Fund short sellers.

Jeff Greene spilled the beans, and confessed the whole scam, when he confessed the truth on TV and said that they were taking bets pending government regulations, if the regulators move to change the rules in their favor, they will make a lot of money on previously loosing positions. Managed Funds Association members, the Hedge Fund short sellers, have already unduly influenced the regulators. They have already taken care of the regulators, so it was somewhat a safe bet. So there you have it. They cheated, lobbied behind the scene to subvert the system and change the rules of the game, in the middle of the game. They turned their loosing positions into profitable trades, defrauded the banking industry and their share holders and in the process they defrauded America and looted all the publicly traded companies and their shareholders and retirement portfolios and 401k portfolios. They took everybody's money, crashed the market torpedoed the U.S. economy from a normal slow down and continued growth and expansion into a deeper recession, heading into a depression. They undermined America and free market capitalism. They wrecked the U.S economy and the housing market causing a liquidity crisis, and a lending freeze, and created an economic crisis. Obama got elected President.

Jeff Greene spilled the beans and told the truth. He confessed and confirmed the scam. He was an innocent participant who benefited from the scam perpetrated by Managed Funds Association members, the Hedge Fund short sellers. Only the guilty are afraid. Jeff Greene was not afraid but was very happy to tell the truth and share the story of his good fortune. Only the guilty are afraid.

John Paulson on the other hand is one guilty looting bandit, a member of managed funds Association, the financial market policy and regulations writing manipulators; A Wizard of Wall Street. John Paulson ridden with guilt, donated $15 million dollars to a group lobbying for judges to be able to modify home mortgages for innocent Americans whom he handed a balance sheet problem as a result of their scam

John Paulson was invited to testify on the hill in early 2009 along with the other looting bandits regarding their thoughts about regulating the Hedge Fund industry. I say he was really nervous, after they had just scammed the banking industry, crashed the market, and looted the country. Only the guilty are afraid, he could not even speak up when he was at the hill to testify on regulating the Hedge Fund industry. He had to throw a celebration party after surviving that hearing.

 Paulson is reported to have made $3.5 billion, and I doubt that. There is still a whole lot of money missing, unaccounted for. He said it was a $10 trillion dollar pot, nobody has been reported making any thing close to the money they should have made from the down turn, especially having been their in the very beginning, shorting the housing market, the banks and the financials. One should multiply that $3.5 billion by 10, which would be more like it, and that, would give you $35 billion dollars.
His portfolio has to be up over 600% unless the $35 billion dollar fund is the fund size after the crisis, then their figures would be correct.

Same thing applies to George Soros. If the fund size estimate is calculated after the crisis, then his figures may be right; otherwise, I am skeptical.

Some Hedge Fund short sellers who arrived late in shorting the housing market, and were net short, going into the financial melt down saw their portfolio gain more than 600%, for example Jeff Greene, the California real estate mogul I mentioned above. So, I don't see how John Paulson and George Soros could not have seen more than a 600% gain in their portfolios as well. They both may be understating their gains during the crisis for fear of engendering public anger. Only the guilty are afraid.

I wonder why someone like George Soros would send their propaganda team and their media spokespersons to appear on TV to publicize how small the money they made from the crisis was, unless they wanted to misinform and mislead the public, so as not to raise public suspicion or anger regarding their loot.

I suspect that George Soros may have made closer to $11 billion dollars from the economic crisis, instead of the one billion dollars his media machine publicized. Again, that depends upon when the fund size was calculated, whether it was before or after the market crash.

Hedge Fund short sellers are very secretive, so I cannot state for certain, how much money they made, they will not even disclose who their clients are. However, whatever they made was obtained through dirty tactics and scam. To really find out the truth, they need to be regulated and investigated.

The Hedge Fund industry needs to be regulated and the Hedge Fund short sellers who were involved in the scam need to be investigated.

Well I digressed a bit there.

Back to what I was saying earlier.

CONSOLIDATION OF POWER CONTINUES

If Managed Funds Association perceives someone to be influential, to be an important personality, or an important adversary, or a potential adversary, or had an important position in government, they will snag the person in to work for them

Managed Funds Association members and their alliances are the masters of corruption, contaminating, compromising and manipulating the influential talent pool.

They have now even gone after our national economist, Alan Greenspan, a voice that could be trusted, a voice that could speak up against them. Today Alan Greenspan works for them through John Paulson.   John Paulson, member Managed Funds Association recently retained the consulting services of Alan Greenspan.

Like I said before, the influence of Managed Funds Association is far reaching and extensive, encompassing the media as well. They claim to be, and they are the primary source of information for policy makers and the media. They feed the financial news media with misinformation, disinformation, market moving news, market moving tips, and sometimes market moving rumors, talking up their books. The financial news media validates and lends credibility to the lies of members of Managed Funds Association and validates their misinformation and disinformation; that is how the truth about what caused the economic crisis has been suppressed; the media goes to them (members of MFA) for commentary.

Managed Funds Association is very powerful and influential. Their influence is far reaching, extensive and complete. Their influence extends into the White House advisory committee. They are influential in political appointments with or without the administration being clued in. They are everywhere, globally positioned to manipulate and exert influence from abroad; manufacturing the appearance of a consensus through cooperative alliances and strategic partnerships they developed. The policy makers and regulators adopt their recommendations and make it into law.

In American today, Managed Funds Association is the establishment. With their tentacles wrapped around the Obama's banking and financial market regulations and CIA politics they operate as though they are the shadow government. And for all intended purposes, in function and in essence, they are the shadow government, the secret government within the Obama government administration. Their most influential and leading members and their alliances are the oligarchies. They have a choke hold on our financial system and the stock market. They have a choke hold on our economy, and in extension, they have a choke hold on America. They have the ears of the president of United States of America. They have the ears of President Obama. He listens to them, and just like the policy makers and the regulators, he adopts their recommendations into his new policies too. He too is a Washington lap dog, beholden to George Soros, the Hedge Fund short seller, the wizard of Wall Street. Consequentially, President Obama, is being deceived, misinformed and misdirected by his key advisors, the ones with connection to Managed Funds Association members, the Hedge Fund short sellers.

All the banking and financial market regulators and policy makers including the White House, the Senate and Congress, all those that listen to and adopt regulations and policy recommendations from the Managed Funds Association, are all lap dogs of the Hedge Funds short sellers.

Our democracy is gradually dying, when the elected officials do not honor the will of the people. They do whatever Managed Funds Association will pay them to do. Our democracy is gradually morphing into a socialist style oligarchy headed by members of Managed Funds Association.

Managed Funds Association members supported and raised money for the Obama campaign. Their members plotted and succeeded in defrauding the banking industry and their shareholders. They manufactured and created the economic crisis that got Barack Obama elected, while they looted America in the process.

Does Obama know anything about their scheme and crime? No. I do not think so. Of course not, he thinks he won by his power of persuasion through speeches and political campaign. Obama does not know anything about their crime. Obama does not even know what caused the economic crisis. He did not know what caused the economic crisis during the presidential campaign and he still does not know what caused the economic crisis even until today.
Eight years of George W. Bush did not cause this economic crisis.

During the 2008 presidential election campaign, Barack Obama was blaming eight years of George W. Bush as the reason for the economic crisis.
What President Obama knows today as being the reason for the economic crisis is what Managed Funds Association members in his administration have told him.
Excuse me, the same people who engineered the economic collapse, crashed the stock market, and looted every portfolio that had exposure to the stock market; in excess of $11 trillion in the biggest scam and fraud in human history are in the White House? They have been given a seat at the table. They are running the country. They are getting away with murder, and getting away with the loot.

The same people who manufactured the economic crisis and looted America are writing the recovery plan, including all banking and financial market regulatory reforms. And that is the reason why you are never going to hear the honest solution to this economic crisis from the Obama administration, because his key advisors were appointed by the looters, Managed Funds Association members. His key advisors were selected by the wizards of Wall Street.

80

The Obama administration key advisors selected by Managed Funds Association through strategic planning are John Podesta, the head of the Obama transition team; Larry summers his chief economic advisor; Tim Geithner his treasury secretary; and Mary Schapiro, his SEC Chairman. They are all lap dogs, the Washington lap dogs of the manipulating Hedge Fund short sellers; the wizards of Wall Street.

The Geithner bank rescue plan is written by the Hedge Fund short sellers. It created an avenue for them to wash their loot through a joint investment with the government in which they will leverage with a government guarantee to buy the bank's assets which they have artificially driven down the value. The Government will allow them to leverage the buying power equivalent of $1 million dollars for every $60 thousand dollars they invested and the government will also guarantee their $60 thousand dollar investment. But you need to have access to $10 billion dollars to qualify to participate. The looting of America still continues with the backing of the U.S. Government, it is just another reward for the looting bandits, the Hedge Fund short sellers, for their support of Barack Obama during the presidential election campaign, utilizing the same leveraging they blamed the banks and insurance companies for having caused the economic crisis in the first place. What a tangled web they have weaved.

Leveraging or poor risk management was not the cause of the economic crisis. Neither bankers, insurance companies nor the borrowers caused the economic crisis. All the regulatory reforms, concentrating on risk management, are still part of Managed Funds Association misinforming and misdirecting the administration. No new regulation is needed. They just need to reinstate all the regulations that Managed Funds Association lobbied to have removed. Put back all the regulations they removed, and that will solve the economic crisis and restore investor confidence.

During the campaign Obama blamed Republicans for deregulation. Why is he not putting back the same regulations that he blamed the Republicans for removing? Let me guess the answer, Obama thought about putting back the regulations but his advisors, who were hand picked by Managed Funds Association, Tim Gethner, Larry Summers, and Mary Schapiro told him, no you do not need to put them back. Those rules were really very old and outdated. Those rules were 72 years old, outdated and are not compatible with the modern computers and system we have now. It will be structurally impossible to implement those rules with the electronics and modern computers we use now. You, Mr. President, the wise one, you need to come up with some new rules for the 21st century. We will help you with that. So they wrote the new regulations for him. (They lie to him, Just bunch of lies from dirty liars). Yes, that conversation probably was something like that, and Obama fell for it.

(Unless, President Obama is deliberately delaying to reinstate the rules immediately, but waiting to first implement all of his very ambitious agenda, like his non stimulating gigantic stimulus package, free government health care reform, cap and trade legislation, the card check bill, more punitive taxation of the so called rich, and the appointment of a union representative to every corporate board room in America if he can, before he reinstates the safeguard regulations, so that he can claim that it was his new policies that were responsible for the economic recovery. That scenario will be consistent with his advisors telling him not to waste a good crisis, meaning they are not going to reinstate the safeguard regulations removed by Christopher Cox until they accomplish all the administration's legislative agendas first. Hold the economic recovery hostage until you pass all your agenda through congress and the senate, and then reinstate the safeguard regulations and give the country the economic recovery).

I will say it again; quite simple, no new regulations are needed. Just put back the old ones that were removed. They served us well for 72 years without a great stock market crash or a depression. Once Christopher Cox and Managed Funds

Association members, the Hedge Fund short sellers, removed the safeguard regulations, the market crashed, and we sank into a depression. And that was not a coincidence.

Once you know the facts, you will come to the proper conclusion and solution. Bush, Reagan, Clinton, the bankers, you and me, insurance companies, lenders, borrowers, poor people, rich people, American consumers, over leveraging, poor risk management, Alan Greenspan, Country Wide nor AIG, caused this economic crisis. They were all victims. We are all victims of this economic crisis created by Managed Funds Association members and their alliances.

All the reasons the media propaganda of Managed Fund Association members, cited for the cause of the economic crisis were actually all the vital, integral path of our capitalist economic growth engine. Securitization in structured finance is a major source of economic growth and expansion, and so are lending, finance and borrowing. Without which there will not be the robust American economic growth and expansion that was the envy of the whole world.

The removal of the safeguard regulations was meant to strip the capitalist economy of its protection, and the introduction of mark-to-market accounting was done to hasten its demise, and it was all a scam, orchestrated by the wizards of Wall Street, sanctioned and promulgated into the law by their Washington lap dogs. As a result, the banking industry and their shareholders were defrauded, and America was looted by members of Managed Funds Association all of whom are Hedge Fund short sellers, whom I have chosen to call the "wizards of Wall Street". Notable among them are Jim "the lying snake" Chanos, George Soros, John Paulson, Kenneth Griffin, David Shaw, James Simon, Philip Falcone, Paul Tudor Jones, Alec Litowitz and a host of others.

The entire membership of Managed Funds Association, were all participants in the looting of America, in various degrees, each member according to the size of the portfolio they were managing.

The lobbyist that made it all happen, the intermediaries that interfaced with the Washington lap dogs were Eric Vincent, John G. Gaine, and Richard Baker.

Richard baker was a former Republican Congress man, the toughest critic of the Hedge Fund short sellers when he was in the house financial services committee, whom Managed fund Association hired as their executive President and paid him millions of dollars to use his influence to gain access to, and mislead some members of the Bush Administration particularly, Christopher Cox, his former colleague from the house of Congress.

So, the people that caused the economic crisis were all members of Managed Funds Association, the Hedge Fund short sellers. They lobbied to remove, and succeeded in removing all the safeguard regulations that protected risk taking and capitalism, and succeeded in removing the regulations that protected all the publicly traded companies and their shareholders.

 The removal of the uptick rule, the removal of the circuit breakers, the removal of trading curbs (all safeguard regulations) and the suspension of historic cost accounting method for the banks and financial institutions and the introduction of mark-to-market accounting (a destructive regulation) by Christopher Cox at SEC, at the request of the Hedge Fund short sellers through Managed Funds Association is what caused the economic crisis.

Managed Funds Association members through their media spokespersons wants America to believe that the crisis is self inflicted due to our economic life style of borrowing and financing.

The only reason why, and the cause of the economic crisis is the removal of the safeguard regulation that protected risk taking and capitalism, which Managed Funds Association members and their alliances, the Hedge Fund short sellers,

Jim Chanos, John Paulson, George Soros, Richard Baker, Eric Vincent, John G. Gaine, and others lobbied to remove, and succeeded in removing, which allowed them to loot the banking industry and their shareholders and looted America in the process.

All the leading Hedge Fund short sellers and members of Managed Fund Association founders' council were all involved in the scam to defraud the banking industry and their shareholders, because they formulated the strategy of lobbying the SEC to remove all the 1938 safeguard regulations and bring back an accounting regulation, previously abolished in 1938 for having caused several bank failures called mark-to-market accounting, so that, they can re-create conditions similar to the 1929 era, which resulted in the great Stock Market Crash of 1929 and the Great Depression. Consequently, when the similar conditions existing in the 1929 era is re-created through the regulatory changes they will obtain, the bank stock prices will fall, many banks will fail, the stock market will crash, the Hedge Fund short sellers will make a ton of money reaping huge profits, the economy will collapse, the country will slide into a depression, they will blame the bankers and borrowers and bad risk management, and there will be massive job losses, bankruptcy, foreclosures, rising unemployment, fear and hopelessness. The people will be angry at their government and want a change in hope of a better tomorrow and If they can get their own candidate elected as president, there will be no investigation because they will have the reigns of power, the power of the presidency, the money, the control of the financial market and national economy, and practically own the country Nobody will be investigated, no body will go to jail. It will be a perfect crime it will be a perfect scam it will be a government by Hedge Fund short sellers for Hedge Fund short sellers. It will be an oligarchy. Their power will be consolidated, complete and absolute.
No more United States of America, but United Shorts of America; the short sellers' paradise and utopia. They got to be crazy.

THE WEASEL

Managed Fund Association and their strategic partners with the corporation of Christopher Cox at the SEC, caused the economic crisis. Notable institutions (conspirators) who are the strategic partners of MFA are: the NYSE, CME, EUREX, Goldman Sachs, UBS AG, Morgan Stanley, Credit Suisse, Deutsche bank securities, JP Morgan chase and others

Managed Funds Association members and their strategic partners and alliances rendered their financial and political support to Obama during the campaign. As part of their grand scheme, MFA weaseled and slithered their way into his campaign, into his administration and into the White House.

The culminating point of his life's work, George Soros said; He created an economic crisis, got his candidate elected and got richer in doing so. He was having a good crisis; it is the culminating point of his life's work.

Did Obama choose Managed Funds Association members and their strategic partners and alliances for support? No. While Obama knew of George Soros, he does not know or care about what trade organization George Soros belonged to: Obama did not solicit the support of Managed Funds Association. He does not even know that they exist. Obama was introduced to Managed Funds Association members by George Soros.

THE KING MAKER

In 2004, Obama was recognized as the rising star among democratic politicians. George Soros and Obama met in 2004 when George Soros raised money for the Obama U.S. Senate campaign.

Before the Democratic Party presidential primary really got on the way, with their plan to eviscerate and obliterate all the depression era safeguard regulations in the works, (in progress) George Soros had to pick his candidate for his second attempt to win the White House.

George Soros vetted, interviewed and picked Barack Obama, then introduced him to the members of Managed Funds Association.

George Soros chose Obama because of his far left ignorance, artless, gullible, credulity, and naivety. He chose Obama because of his far left radical ideology, and his lack of experience, and lack of knowledge of economics and financial markets. He would be easier to deal with, easier to influence or manipulate. He would be easier to deal with than a Hillary Clinton. And of course Obama had charisma.

George Soros in his New York Office in 2006 introduced Barack Obama to Orin Kramer and Robert Wolf. Orin Kramer is a Hedge Fund manager. Robert Wolf is the president of UBS investments. Both men are members of Managed Funds Association. Both men became the key operators of the Obama juggernaut, the Obama campaign fundraiser and bundling money machine.
George Soros also introduced Obama to Paul Tudor Jones, of Tudor Investment Corporation, and both men hosted a

fundraiser for Obama. Tudor Investments Corporation is a member of Managed Funds Association.
Jim Chanos of Kynikos Associates, the Hedge Fund short sellers in chief, also raised money for Obama. All were members of Managed Funds Association.

George Soros put the support of the organization behind Obama. Members of Managed Funds Association, the Hedge Funds short sellers supported and financed Barack Obama's campaign, with George Soros as the King Maker in Chief.

George Soros chose Obama. He could have chosen Hillary Clinton, but he did not. He wanted somebody that hates the traditional America, and its constitutions, a left wing radical, like himself, so he chose Barack Obama. The far left grass root organizations which were being funded by George Soros also preferred a candidate Barack Obama over candidate Hillary Clinton. They trusted Obama more to champion their far left ignorance and ideology, the anti war, George Bush derangement syndrome, lets-blame-America-first-movement.

Managed Funds Association members supported Obama. They are the King makers. They are the masters of puppets. With their grand scheme of creating an economic crisis in mind, and putting fear in the hearts of the electorates, anyone they chose could have won.
They chose Obama, and they were very comfortable with his lack of experience, lack of knowledge of economics and financial markets; his artless gullible credulity: He will be more susceptible to their influence, manipulations, lies and deceit. Managed Funds Association will consolidate their power and establish an oligarchy, the shadow government, the secret government within the Obama government administration. George Soros will be influential and can implement his world view and far left radical socialist agenda through legislative and regulatory reforms. Obama will be under the tutelage of the members of Managed Funds Association, he will be learning from them, more trusting, and will not suspect a thing, or go after them or try to investigate or prosecute them. After all, during the campaign Obama thought that the economic

crisis was caused by trickle down economics from President Reagan that finally failed during the eight years of George Bush. He did not know the truth then and he still does not know the truth today, because he has surrounded himself with representatives of the plotters, the looting bandits, Managed Funds Association members. Oh, excuse me; it is the other way around: Obama does not even know the truth about what caused the economic crisis, because the plotters, the perpetrators, the looting bandits, Managed Funds Association members, have surrounded him, and they have his ears. They are the King makers. The puppet masters, the wizards of Wall Street have the ear of the President of the United States. And they are misleading, misinforming and misdirecting him. They have the ear of the President of the United States. They have Obama's ears.

Now when Managed Fund Association member George Soros makes a comment about how Obama missed an opportunity on properly dealing with the banking crisis, Obama adjusts his policy on dealing with the banks.

When George Soros mentions that the former Bush Administration members should be prosecuted for torture, Obama adjusts and shifts his decision on the issue, from leaving the past behind and looking forward to the future, to kicking the ball down to his attorney general to prosecute those who are responsible. Maybe it is all a coincidence, or great minds thinking alike? No, I don't think so. John Podesta is the link between George Soros ideas and Barack Obama's shifting policies.
John Podesta made the request on behalf of Soros, to prosecute former Bush administration officials who will be accused of being responsible for torturing enemy combatants.

Managed Funds Association had their point man in the Obama campaign. And they were in the Obama transition team, and were influential in key appointments relating to the economy and the financial markets. John Podesta, now a Lobbyist, sponsored by George Soros, member Managed Funds Association was the head of Obama's transition team.

Managed Fund Association member Orin Kramer is Obama's chief fundraiser; the chief campaign fund bundler.

Larry Summers, from D.E. Shaw & Co, a member of Managed Funds Association is Obama's national economic advisor.

Jim Chanos, the premier national short seller in chief, a key player and schemer, a member of Managed Fund Association alliance, is an Obama fundraiser, the Hedge Fund short seller in chief.

When Jim Chanos writes a 500,000.00 dollar check for Obama, what do you think he is paying for? What do you think he is buying? How about being considered beyond suspicion and beyond reproach status? How about immunity from investigation before you can even think or talk about prosecution?

When D.E Shaw & Co, a member of Managed Funds Association writes Larry Summers a check for $5.2 million dollars, what do you think they want in return? How about influence, less regulation, misdirecting and misinforming the President as to the reason for the economic crisis? How about acceptances, and being above suspicion, and reproach, comes what may, immunity from investigation?

The Hedge Fund short sellers' tie to the Obama administration is pervasive. As a matter of fact, the Hedge Fund short sellers' tie to democratic policy makers, committee chairs, and regulators is crippling to a true representative government for the people by the people. It is now, a government by Hedge Fund short sellers for Hedge Fund short sellers, an oligarchy. The wizards of Wall Street and their Washington lap dogs gorging themselves at the expense of the American people.

The policy makers and regulators out sources the banking and financial institution's regulations and policies, to the Hedge Funds short sellers, and then rubber stamp, validate and adopts their recommendation into the law.

Yes our policy makers and regulators out sources all banking and financial market regulations to the Hedge Fund short sellers at Managed Funds Association, and the Hedge Fund short sellers will write all the new policies and regulations, and the policy makers and regulators will then, rubber stamp and approve their recommendation, and it becomes the law.

By the time this book gets published, if it gets published, and when it gets published, you can take the information revealed in its passages, and verify the source of various banking and financial institution regulations, policies and plans adopted during the Obama administration. You will find the finger prints of Managed Funds Association members and their alliances all over it.

You will find out, that these regulations, policies and plans, were all written by Hedge Fund short sellers, and originated from Hedge Fund short sellers, members of the founders' council and sustaining members of Managed Funds Association and their point men in the Obama administration. We have a government by Hedge Fund short sellers for Hedge Fund short sellers, by Managed Funds Association, the lobbying company for the Hedge Funds short sellers, an oligarchy, the shadow government, the secret government within the Obama government administration.

 The Obama zero tolerance policy for lobbyist, made an exception for lobbyist who can bring improvement to our national economy and stock market structure. That sounds like an exception, or a loop hole, to accommodate the members of Managed Funds Association, the very same lobbying company, and its members, the Hedge Fund short sellers, the looting bandits, who created this economic crisis, who plotted and defrauded the banking industry and their shareholders and wrecked the national economy, and looted every publicly traded company and its shareholders, 401k investors, common investors and retirement portfolio, and gave all American consumers a national balance sheet problem.
They are now in the White House. They are now running the country. A government by Hedge Fund short sellers, for Hedge Fund short sellers. The bad Wall Street with all of its

negative connotations and attributes as I described earlier, is now running the government. We now have a casino economy, and socialism, in the making.

Through D.E Shaw & CO, member Managed Funds Association, Larry summer received a $5.2 million dollar consulting contract, and, $2.7 million in speaking fees from other affiliated financial institutions. Larry Summer has the ear of the president of United States. Larry Summers, Has Obama's ear.

Managed Funds Association, through their White House, inside track point man and Head of the Obama transition team, John Podesta, were influential in presidential appointments. They influenced both the appointment of Mary Schapiro to head the SEC, and Tim Geithner, to head the treasury department.
Their man at the treasury is Tim Geithner.

Managed Funds Association members, the Hedge Fund short sellers, the cabal of slithery rich vultures wrote the Geithner bank rescue plan of public private investment partnership program. A convenient way for the Hedge Fund short sellers to wash all the money they had stolen. It allows them to utilize the same leveraging, which they criticized the bankers and insurers for using, as being the reason for the economic crisis.

Managed Funds Association members, the Hedge Fund short sellers, the cabal of slithery rich serpents, the cabal of slithery rich vultures will write the new banking and financial market regulatory reform, and will continue to be the source of all our economic, banking and financial market regulations and policies for the foreseeable future, unless this truth about what caused the economic crisis is revealed.

Unless the truth about the role of Managed Funds Association in our government policies and regulations is revealed, and some courageous lawmakers for country, duty, and honor free our economic system from their grip, this nation is in for a long time of hurt and a possible bankruptcy.

The activities of the cabal of slithery rich vultures at the Managed Funds Association; the Wizard of Wall Street must be exposed, investigated, and held accountable for their dirty deeds and crime, tried, and when convicted, be put in jail.

There is always a glaring contradiction between the reasons the Hedge Fund short sellers' media propaganda gave as the reason for the economic crisis, and the solutions, and additional investment products that they are introducing.

They blamed leveraging, borrowing and over extension of credit for having caused the economic crisis, yet their solution for toxic mortgage assets calls for more leveraging and borrowing and extension of credit. That goes to show that the practices employed by the bankers did not cause the economic crisis but rather encouraged and fostered economic growth.

The government by Hedge Fund short sellers, coming up with the same system of finance and leveraging as was being used by the banks, in the Tim Geithner bank rescue plan, goes to show that they lied about leveraging and borrowing being the cause of the economic crisis.
You can not have an economic growth and expansion with out credit, lending and borrowing.

America operates on credit. Our economic system is capitalism in which wealth and method of producing wealth is privately owned, operated and traded for profit. That trading aspect of capitalism is facilitated by credit and financing where private equity ownership appreciating in value overtime, attracts investment capital through capital formation.
The people who provide the funds, the people who provide the capital for financing growth, must be protected from those who want to steal their capital and funds through crooked means or fraud. They must be protected from the short sellers. They must be protected from the Hedge Fund short sellers, who seek to take away liquidity (capital) from those who provide the liquidity. They must be protected by having regulations

that prevents fraud and price manipulation, by having regulations that allow for invested capital to appreciate in value, and encourage capital formation, by having regulations that governs short sale transactions to protect our capitalist system and those who invest in it; the publicly traded companies and their shareholders; private equity ownership. There is no capitalism unless the capital is legally protected.

The bankers, insurance companies or the American consumers, borrowers, poor people, the lenders, Wall Street executives, did not cause this economic crisis. They were all operating within the safety net that our capitalist economic and financial system provided them as a result of the depression era regulations, put in place in 1938, to allow assets to appreciate in value, fostering growth and attracting more investments. The depression era regulations protected capitalism and investors: it allowed for capital to appreciate and encouraged capital formation; the capital needed for economic growth and job creation.

The bankers, insurers, American consumers, 30 years of Reaganomics, George W. Bush, and all that were blamed, or accused of causing this economic crisis were all victims of the back room dealing by the Hedge Fund short sellers, who lobbied and legally bribed regulators to change the rules that safeguarded our capitalist economic and financial system put in place to protect the system, the common investors from the short sellers.
The regulations were put in place to protect investors from the likes of Managed Funds Association members, the Hedge Fund short sellers. But the SEC let the fox in to guard the hen house, or say, they let the wolves in to guard the sheep, because the wolves - Hedge Fund short sellers were in the sheep clothing.

Managed Funds Association members and their alliances ,the Hedge Fund short sellers caused this economic crisis for shorting profits and for some key members, the key plotters they had other ulterior motives which was to create an economic crisis to guarantee the election of Barack Obama.

The mastermind with the ulterior motive of creating an economic crisis to guarantee the election of Barack Obama was George Soros, and he did get richer in doing so.

So.
They looted America, and they are still looting America amidst the chaos they created. Yes, the chaos they created.

According to George Soros, his comments after the markets, and the economy has collapsed, in the middle of the depression, after Barack Obama was already sworn in as president, George Soros said, I quote " Life is generated at the edge of chaos, so I specialize in this edge of chaos. I am having a good crisis; it is in a way the culmination point of my life's work, It has been stimulating." end of quote.

A man that revels in chaos, I will say is essentially evil.
A man that revels in chaos, enjoying our national economic crisis in which some people actually died as result of what he created, which he finds to be very stimulating, and he described it as the culminating point of his life's work is definitely evil. George Soros couldn't help himself. He had to brag and boast about his crime.

Just like all criminals that commit major crimes, even though they don't want to be caught and held responsible for their crimes, they always wants to let people know about their astonishing feat. They always brag, and boast about their crime. And George Soros did so, with the above quote attributed to him.

THE PAPER TRAIL

Managed Funds Association members and their alliances should be investigated for their role in creating this economic crisis and their looting of America, and to unduly influence the outcome of 2008 Presidential election through manipulation of the emotions of fear.

The investigation would reveal all their lobbying activities, all their short selling trading activities, and how their shorting activities corresponded to the several bank failures and frequent stock market crashes, leading up to the presidential election. The investigation should reveal that they are common criminals after all. They are thieves.

The investigation should reveal the individual moves the key players were making, the details of the meeting between John Paulson and Harvey Pitt.
John Paulson said he hired Harvey Pitt former SEC chairman to spread the word about Bear sterns planning to manipulate the market.
My question is, spread the word to whom? Who is Harvey Pitt going to spread the word to? The SEC or the accounting board FASB?

My translation: John Paulson hired Harvey Pitt former SEC chairman as an emissary to help lobby his former colleagues at the SEC and FASB to remove the safeguard regulations and bring back mark-to-market accounting.

The investigation should reveal the details of the meeting between George Soros and John Paulson, What information was exchanged, what corresponding action they took afterwards, details of their trading positions and trading accounts records leading to the removal of the safeguard regulations and introduction of mark-to-market accounting.

The investigation should reveal Details of their trading account records through the frequent stock market crashes leading up to the presidential election.

The investigation should reveal details of the meeting between Jim Chanos and Christopher Cox. The investigation should reveal all Jim Chanos trading account records leading to the dates the regulations were removed through the frequent stock market crashes leading to the presidential election.

The investigation should reveal all the secrets of Managed Funds Association members, the Hedge Fund short sellers. and their alliances. All the secrets held in the trading account records of the leading Hedge Funds short sellers and members of Managed Funds Association's sustaining members and founder's council like James Simon, Renaissance technologies, Kenneth Griffin, Citadel investment David Shaw, D E Shaw & Co, John Paulson, Paulson & co, Alec Litowitz, Magnetar Capital and the masterminds: Hedge Fund short seller in chief, Jim Chanos and George Soros. Of course, they will claim they are innocent of any wrong doing. Well, all they need to do is disclose all their lobbying activities and open up their account trading records.

For Managed Fund Association members and their alliances to disclose their trading account record activities is all they really need to do, to prove their innocence and lack of involvement in defrauding the banking industry and their shareholders, and looting America in the process, and creating an economic crisis that did put fear in the hearts of the electorate which resulted in the election of Barack Obama. The American public will like to know the truth, and therefore should demand a transparency of Managed Funds Association members trading activities surrounding the crucial dates mentioned above. The American public through their representatives should demand transparency of all the Hedge Fund short sellers trading activities.

Managed Fund Association members and their alliances, the Hedge Fund Short sellers should not have any problem to provide factual data to exonerate themselves, and prove that they were not the looting bandits. They should welcome an open transparent disclosure of their trading activities around the critical dates mentioned above, and also disclose all their lobbying activities, phone records and email correspondence. My guess is that, Managed Funds Association members and their alliances will rather pay Barack Obama $1billion dollars, Harry Reid $1 billion dollars, and Nancy Pelosi $1 billion dollars each, to block any investigation, rather than release this very crucial information needed to prove their innocence.

This is the same Hedge Fund short sellers who wanted accounting transparency from the bankers and financial institutions. This is the same Hedge Fund short sellers who went to regulators and policy makers and misrepresented themselves to the SEC and FASB as investors and wanted accounting regulations changed for the protection of investors and for investor transparency. They do not want to be transparent in any of their own investment activities. They are very secretive.

They are very secretive on whom their clients are. Very secretive on what their investment positions, or portfolios are. They do not want any prying eyes, or be regulated. They are always lying and cheating and slithering their way through Washington. And now, they are lying and cheating, deceiving, and slithering their way through the White House and the nation.

Their ideas are dripping into the Obama administration policy. They are rewriting all our economic and financial regulatory rules. They are essentially running the country period. Creating a government by scam and shifting policies.

Managed Funds Association members and their alliances created this economic crisis, lobbied for, and succeeded in removing all the safeguard regulations that protected capitalism; they removed all the safeguard regulations that protected all the publicly traded companies and their shareholders. Now they collude to manipulate and loot the stock market. They lobbied successfully to bring back an accounting regulations previously abolished for having caused several bank failures, called mark-to-market accounting and they imposed it on the banks and financial institutions, causing several banks to fail, wrecked a havoc on the stock market and on all the publicly traded companies, causing panic share declines through collusion and stock price manipulation, bear raided and looted the banks and all the publicly traded companies and their shareholders.

They have looted America and they are still looting America through misleading the administration, edging the country closer and closer to socialism. These are the people that have Obama's ear. These are the people the White House and the administration is listening to and heeding their counsel.

The Obama administration listens to George Soros, and may adopt George Soros solution for resolving the banking balance sheet crisis, which is a government take over of the banks through converting the government preferred shares into common shares, or fire sale them to MFA members.

George Soros is a member of Managed Funds Association. George Soros is a member of the founder's council at Managed Fund Association. George Soros is the secret hand that got Obama Elected. The lobbying company that represents George Soros and the other Hedge Fund short sellers is called Managed Funds Association; they lobbied the SEC to remove the safeguard regulations that protected capitalism, our publicly traded companies and their shareholders.

George Soros is the puppet master; the chief wizard of Wall Street and John Podesta is his puppet string; the conduit and link between George Soros and the White House.

George Soros is the most influential democratic political power player. He has spent more than $100 million dollars on courses supporting liberal democratic agenda.

He is the man that spent $20 million dollars to defeat George Bush in favor of John Kerry for the control of the SEC.

He has contributed or raised $18 million dollars to groups seeking campaign finance reform that advantaged George Soros to contribute to the Obama campaign.

He has contributed or raised $15 million dollars to left wing organizations seeking the defeat of Bush.

He has contributed or raised $5 million dollars to Move on .org in an effort to defeat bush.

George Soros is the man behind the money that elected Barack Obama. George Soros is a man with a history of market manipulation. An investigation of Managed Funds Association will reveal a dirty can of worms; make that a can of snakes. What does George Soros want from a President John Kerry? Control of the SEC as it was written, in 2004.

Did George Soros finally get his revenge in defeating a Bush like McCain?

Of course he did. Is George Soros a member of Managed Fund Association?

Yes he is.

Is George Soros part of the Cabal? Yes he is.

Does George Soros know the reason for the great Stock Market Crash of 1929 and the cause of the Great Depression? Yes he does.

Is George Soros a Hedge Fund short seller? Yes he is. Does George Soros relish a stock market crash if he has a short position? Yes he does.

Did George Soros through Managed Funds Association and their alliances and emissaries lobby the SEC and FASB to remove the uptick rule, the circuit breakers, the trading curb, and impose mark-to-market accounting regulations on the banks and financial institutions exposed to the sub prime and option arm mortgage? Yes he did. Did George Soros short the housing market, the banking industry, sub prime mortgages and option arm mortgages? Yes he did.

Did George Soros profit from the economic crisis? Yes he did. Did his candidate win the election? Yes he did. Did his candidate benefit from the economic crisis to get elected? Yes he did. Is George Soros happy about the economic crisis? Yes he is. He couldn't control himself that he had to reveal that he was having a good crisis; he described it as the culminating point of his life's work.

CONCLUSION

So what should President Obama do?

In February when Obama, first took office, if he knew what had happened. He should have followed the money, because there are paper trails, which will lead him to the looters. He should have, just like an impartial referee sounded his foul whistle, and stopped all the players on their tracks.
And like a referee, he should have put the looters in a penalty box, and asked the lines man, the brokerages to reset all the trading accounts to what they were on July 6th 2007 when they removed the uptick rule, and then tell the looters to return all the monies, and put the monies back into the trading accounts. That one move would have reverberated favorably for America around the world for centuries to come. All the people affected here at home, and around the world, would have been positively affected and made whole again, and the global confidence in America will be permanent, and indisputable. It was very possible to do this very early, before the monies got mingled in various transactions. It may be already too late to still do that now. I do not know.

So Obama did not know what caused the economic crisis then, and he still does not know what caused it today, because the looters have surrounded him and are misinforming, misdirecting and misleading him.
But when the truth eventually comes out as a result of my efforts or the efforts of anyone willing to help, and step up to tell the truth, what then should President Obama do?

He still can see if it is possible for the looters to restore every body's accounts and 401k portfolios. He should definitely eject all the point men representing the looters Managed Funds Association members from his administration. He should hold the looters accountable for their crimes. Put them in hand cuffs and let them stand trial for their crimes and make them

101

return the loot, and follow the money, follow the money paper trail, and recover as much of the stolen loot as possible and still return the money to the brokerage accounts, and restore everyone's portfolios accounts to the best they can.

There is about $11 trillion dollars looted from the publicly traded companies and their shareholders, most of that money if recovered should find their way back into the individual accounts around the globe, here in America and abroad.

But instead, what is going on is that the looters have surrounded Obama. They are embedded in his administration, offering counsel and advice to him: writing new banking and financial markets regulations with their foot on the economic neck of the country, suppressing business freedom, capitalism and economic growth; while they are chumming it up with the President and his cabinet; as the nation continues racking up more debt in trillions upon trillions to replace the stolen money. The people who deliberately engineered the economic collapse and the stock market crash and looted every portfolio that had exposure to the stock market are in the White House.

We are never going to recover from this crisis as long as Obama is listening to the Hedge Fund short sellers. As long as the Hedge Fund short sellers are running the country, and our economy, Obama cannot solve the economic crisis, until he knows the truth about what really happened and uses an executive order to reinstate all the regulations removed under Christopher Cox at the SEC. In essence Obama has to reverse all the regulatory errors of Christopher Cox as I repeatedly stated repeatedly, earlier.

It is difficult to solve a problem if you do not know what the cause of the problem is. And completely impossible to solve the problem, if you are listening to advisors who are purposefully misleading and misdirecting you away from the cause of the problem, and offering you contrary solutions to the problem to avoid culpability and jail time.

All the solutions being offered to Obama by the looters will

make it difficult, if not impossible for us to get out of this economic crisis completely and still be the same capitalist America we knew and loved, and still be the same capitalist America that was both the envy and inspiration to the whole world.
 If you combine the Hedge Fund short sellers ideas, with Obama's none stimulating, gigantic stimulus package, liberal wasteful spending, the cap and trade legislation, and proposed government health care insurance, with mounting national dept, collapsing currency due to unsustainable debt, America could be irreparably destroyed.

The wrong ideas, contrary solution to the economic crisis written by the Hedge Fund short sellers, that the Obama administration is implementing will increase taxes for individuals, small businesses and corporations. It will cause wage deflation, keep personal spending down, punish and discourage risk taking, punish and discourage business investments, business profitability will be less, unemployment will continue to rise, lending will remain low, economic expansion from new business and housing construction will be low, economic growth and expansion from mortgage securitization and structured finance will disappear, economic expansion from lending and credit extension will remain low, Publicly traded companies, and their shareholders, 401k and retirement portfolios will remain vulnerable and unprotected from the Hedge Fund short sellers and broker dealers who collude and manipulate equity prices (stock prices), destroying investment capital and taking away liquidity. Cash and carry economy will replace financial credit extension and lending economy. The country will be at the brink of bankruptcy. And economic power will then permanently shift from the west to the east, with china as the new economic leader.

All the Obama ideas to solve the economic crisis that came from the Hedge Fund short sellers, members of Managed Funds Association are all recipes to destroy capitalism, prolong the recession, and diminish America's economic standing, and permanently alter our economic and financial system and future.

The architects of the economic crisis are the enemies of America; they are members of Managed Funds Association, the Hedge Fund short sellers.

They have an anti-capitalism agenda, an anti-industrialized nation agenda, and a far left liberal, Marxist radical agenda. Hedge Fund short sellers are not capitalist. They are anti-capitalist and they are not investors; they are anti-investors What they are, simply put, are criminals, dirty malicious criminals, evil and diabolic.

One of the quickest ways to make billions of dollars or become a multi-billionaire, other than doing a public offering if you have a viable company with proven track record, is to steal it from the world's richest corporations, the publicly traded companies

The world's socialist dictatorships, military dictatorships and political strong man have done that repeatedly. They seize wealthy corporate assets and become multi-billionaires. They attack capitalism and seize the capitalists' wealthy corporations and nationalize them; loot and steal billions for themselves and become multi-billionaires.

Managed Funds Association, the Hedge Fund short sellers are doing it in America; They looted our wealthiest publicly traded companies and their shareholders, destroyed and collapsed the companies, walked away with the loot, and then return to buy and own the companies for pennies on the dollar, and they are still doing it; looting our wealthiest publicly traded companies and their shareholders; legitimized and sanctioned by their Washington DC Lap dogs, the corrupt elected officials, policy makers and regulators who ceded the power of policy writing and regulatory authority to members of Managed Funds Association, the Hedge Fund short sellers. It is a scandal. It is a coup, and it is corrupt.

The Hedge Fund short sellers, members of Managed Funds Association then writes the laws and regulations, but skew the regulations to undermine our capitalist publicly traded companies by removing the laws that protected the capitalists and their shareholders, by removing the laws that protected their rights to stock equity ownership, and imposing asset devaluating regulations on them such as mark to market accounting regulation, and the removal of the short sale restriction regulation, the uptick rule: leaving the publicly traded capitalist corporations vulnerable and incapable of managing their investment risks, leaving them vulnerable and susceptible to looting through unrestricted short selling by the Hedge Fund short sellers in order to loot them as the regulatory millstone (burden) imposed on them causes the companies to start loosing money, and their stock prices starts to drop, then the Hedge Fund short sellers having opened a short sale position, would make a ton of money; billions when the capitalist company's stock price starts to decline, to the collapse and demise of the capitalist publicly traded company. And that is how the economic crisis was engineered, and that was the scam that elected Barack Obama

Hedge Fund short sellers, members of Managed Funds Association are looting bandits, dirty malicious criminals, evil and diabolical. They are not capitalists. They are criminals. Their leadership and their most influential members are radical far left socialists with Marxist agenda and a diabolical criminal mind.
Managed Fund Association is crafty and deceitful. When they tell you that short selling contributes liquidity to the market, that is a lie; short selling destroys capital and takes away liquidity from the market. When they tell you that they are taking steps to remove manipulation from the stock market, that is a lie, they are taking steps to introduce manipulation to the stock market, and prime the stock market for manipulation and looting. When they tell you that the uptick rule is outdated; because of decimalization, that is a lie. They lie to deceive, to bring forth a big pay day from short selling, hence the looting of America and America's wealthiest corporations and their shareholders, sanctioned by their Washington DC lap dogs.

Managed Funds Association, representing the Hedge Fund short sellers have infiltrated our capitalist system government and have mislead the gullible corrupt policy makers and regulators who had put up their office and influence for sale.

Managed Funds Association paid them for their influence and office, and then took over our government.

The corrupt policy makers and regulators relinquished the power of policy writing and, regulation to the members of Managed Funds Association, the Hedge Fund short sellers and gave them the dominating influence over all policy and regulatory matters concerning our economy, our banking and financial services industry, and our stock market and that was the coup that led to the financial crisis and the economic collapse.

It was a coup that vanquished the capitalist publicly traded companies, and destroyed the real estate industry and devalued our homes, and caused massive unemployment, and retirement portfolios wipe out, job losses, home foreclosures and deaths by suicide. The capitalists' corporations' assets, specifically, the banks' assets and the financial institutions' assets are the mortgage papers to our homes: When Managed Funds Association, the Hedge Fund short sellers started writing regulations that devalued the banks' assets, they were writing regulations that devalued our homes and properties. When they remove regulations that protected our rights to stock equity ownership in order to loot our invested capital in the capitalists' corporations, they were removing the regulation that protected the capital that funded the loans for borrowers, the day to day operations of the corporations, their payroll and the funds they needed for growth and expansion. What ever they did to the banks, the financial institutions, and all the publicly traded companies on Wall Street had repercussions on Main Street; they were doing it to us. We the people are the victims of their plot and scheme. We the people are the victims of their crime.

The dirty malicious scandalous criminal maneuvers of Managed Funds Association members, the Hedge Fund short sellers led to the calamity, the collapse of the economy.

Managed Funds Association is a virus and a cancer to our nation. Managed Funds Association is consuming America from within and consuming America from inside out; exporting their diabolic influence to our European allies sanctioned by their Washington DC lap dogs - the corrupt policy makers and regulators - betrayers of the public trust - pompous arrogant pigs at the trough - the betrayers of the American flag.

The influence of Managed Funds Association has now extended to the British Parliament.

Managed Funds Association has an agenda to undermine the western super powers. They are destroying capitalism. The far left radicals want to pronounce capitalism dead, and a failure. They are misleading our allies, misinforming and misdirecting our European allies, particularly Great Britain. They are working diligently, doing everything possible to cover their role in engineering the economic collapse which have ravaged the American economy and ravaged most of the European economy; they are misleading the western world into an irreparable ruin, stifling the economic recovery and growth; targeting and preying on the capitalist countries and currencies; They operate with impunity and they feel invincible with a license to destroy any company or country; or hold the company or country hostage while preying on the investors. They have dinner meetings, openly discussing collusion to attack a particular asset class, equities, or a country's currency. If this is not organized crime, I do not know what is. Managed Funds Association needs to be abolished.

To fix the economic crisis; along with putting everything back the way they were in 2006 before Christopher Cox started fixing things that were not broken; every regulation that was influenced by Managed Funds Association should be reversed to what it was before, with no exception.
Managed Funds Association is the enemy within; it is the virus and the cancer that is eating away at our democracy, our economic recovery and national defense bit by bit. Gradually but surely, they will inevitably bring this great nation and the western world to its knees unless they are exposed and stopped.

The American people must know the truth about what caused the economic crisis. The American people must know about the role of Managed Funds Association in engineering the economic collapse. The American people must know and reject everything connected with Managed Funds Association; Managed Funds Association has a choke hold on our government. They have a choke hold on our economy. They have a choke hold on our country. I want to be rid of them, and their dominating influence. I want my country back. The American people want their country back, but they need to know from whom to reclaim their country. They need to know about Managed Funds Association.

The elected officials have refused to do anything about Managed Funds Association; they won't lift a finger to investigate them or do anything to curb their dominating influence, because the policy makers and regulators have been bought and paid for by the members of Managed Funds Association.

Elected officials, policy makers and regulators have put their office and influence up for sale and in extension they have put the American government up for sale. And the members of Managed Funds Association have bought our government and the right to write and skew policies and regulations to favor their members at the expense of the American people's interest, at the expense of American national economic interests and at the expense of our national security interest.

They have struck a blow at the heart of capitalism. The heart of capitalism is the individual's right to ownership of wealth. The heart of capitalism is the protection by law, of our God given rights for the individual to own property and wealth. It is called property rights. There are no property rights in socialist countries, and that is one of the big differences between socialism and capitalism. In capitalism we have property rights. In socialism they do not have property rights.

Managed Funds Association, that is, the Hedge Fund short sellers, has attacked capitalism and the invested capital within our capitalist system economy. They have attacked the property rights given to the individuals to own equity in our publicly traded companies. They have attacked the property rights to stock equity ownership

They have removed regulations that protected our invested capital and introduced regulations that devalued our invested capital. We no longer have property rights to the stocks we bought from our publicly traded companies. Short sellers that do not own shares in the publicly traded companies in which we invested in can sell our shares through short selling, to drive down the stock price, putting downward pressure on the stock, to trigger panic selling and panic share price decline unrestricted until the stock price goes down to zero where the company collapses and seizes to exist.
The Hedge Fund short sellers walk away with all our invested capital, stolen from us, sanctioned by their Washington DC lap dogs and no one goes to jail.

The socialist dictators steal by intimidation and seizure. Managed Funds Association; the Hedge Fund short sellers steals by subversion through regulatory changes and price manipulations sanctioned by our government's betrayal of public trust.

Managed Funds Association, the Hedge Fund short sellers attacked capitalism in America. Capitalism is synonymous with America. Capitalism is Americanism.
They attacked and dismantled the underpinnings of capitalism. They are the enemies of the American people. They are the enemies of America. They need to hear from we the people

So I have come to you the American people, when you have completed reading this book, and conducted your own independent investigation, and verified the information contained in this book, and you know in your heart that what you have read is the truth: you must spread the truth about what caused this economic crisis, you must tell your neighbors and friends, and spread the truth about how we got into this mess. Our power lies in numbers. I think when the American people know the truth about how we got into this crisis; they will become as angry as I am about what has happened to our country. There will be a ground swell of public anger, an overwhelming public outcry, enough to make the elected officials act.

If our elected officials do not act, we the people will act and boot them out, all of them but a few, and elect some adults, some American champions to restore the American heritage, legacy and free market capitalism with regulations that protects the value of our homes, with regulations that protects our property rights and ownership of stock equity in our publicly traded companies: and restore a previously reliable pathway to retirement planning and estate planning, knowing your invested assets and capital are protected by law.

For our country, duty and honor, you must do your part to spread this truth to help liberate our country from the clutches of Managed Funds Association. These Washington DC lap dogs won't act unless we the people act.
This cry for freedom and liberty is an emergency cry for help; A cry for help in restoring free market capitalism, a cry for help in restoring America to its heritage and legacy; A cry for help in restoring America to its greatness as the world's leading economic super power.

President Barack Obama, the U.S. Senate and Congress, the Republican party and Democratic party. Can you hear me?
If you want our economy, the real economy, the private sector economy to start growing again, expanding and over heating, you must implement my 7-point action plan solution.
If you want the companies to start hiring again and solve the unemployment problem, you must implement my 7-point action plan solution; you must protect the invested capital needed to create jobs, and protect the value of our assets. You must encourage and protect capitalism and risk taking.

The Chinese economy and the Indian economy are growing, expanding and over heating. They both rejected and banned short selling; their invested capital is protected.
The Australian economy is growing, expanding and over heating. They preserved the short sale restriction regulation; the uptick rule. It was put in place since 1961 and they left it intact; the invested capital and stock equity ownership in Australia are protected by law. Short selling is restricted by regulation. They have rejected Managed Funds Association. Their economy is growing, expanding and over heating.

We the people, we want the restoration of free market capitalism governed by rules and regulation that protects property rights. We want the rules and regulation that protects stock equity ownership, and the invested capital of the investors restored. We want the abolition of Managed Funds Association and the end of their dominating influence in policy writing and regulatory matters. We do not want to hear their opinion, their input or commentary. We want them to cease to exist, abolished and never allowed to regroup or reorganize under a different name. We want them prosecuted, tried and punished. People died, and millions of lives have been displaced and destroyed because of their crime.

We want the control of our country. We want a government that represents the interests of the American people. We want to reclaim our country, and our government from members of Managed Funds Association, the Hedge Fund short sellers.

Those who control the economy, controls the nation and the people within. America is best served if the control of the economy is in the hands of the people, the general public, we the people, and not in the hands of a few, a secret organization, an oligarchy, the members of Managed Funds Association - the Hedge Fund short sellers - led by far left socialist radicals; Diabolic criminals.

Managed Funds Association looms large and appears to be insurmountable; but we will defeat them, because they are thieves and they do not want to be uncovered; we will defeat them because they are guilty, and a poison to our society; and they do not want to be detected. The antidote for ending their dominating influence and defeating them is public awareness of their existence.
Let the American people know about Managed Fund Association and their handy work. The American people will reject their existence. The American people will reject them, cut them out like the cancer which they are, exterminate and abolish them from our society.

Like I stated earlier, America operates on credit. Our economic system is capitalism in which wealth and method of producing wealth is privately owned, operated and traded for profit. That trading aspect of capitalism is facilitated by credit and financing, where private equity ownership appreciates in value over time, by attracting investment capital through capital formation.

The people who provide the funds, the people who provide the capital for financing growth, must be protected from those who want to steal their capital (funds) through crooked means or fraud. The investors must be protected from the short sellers. They must be protected from the Hedge Fund short sellers, those who seek to take away liquidity (capital) from those who provide the liquidity. The investors must be protected by having regulations that prevent fraud and stock price manipulation, by having regulations that allow for invested capital to appreciate in value, and encourage capital formation, by having regulations that governs short sale transactions, to protect our capitalist system and those who invest in it; the publicly traded companies and their shareholders, the private equity ownership, 401k employees, retirement accounts, and the common investors.

President Barack Obama should honor the insight,
and foresight of President Roosevelt and Joe Kennedy.
Joe Kennedy was the SEC Chairman in 1938.
Barack Obama should honor the legacy of Roosevelt and Joe Kennedy, and reinstate all the depression era / Roosevelt regulations that the Hedge Fund short sellers lobbied to have removed in order to properly and correctly solve the economic crisis and prevent a repeat occurrence.
He should restore those Roosevelt and Joe Kennedy regulations to a permanent status and enact a law to recognize those regulations as the safeguards of capitalism, a sacred fabric that binds our economic system together and never to be tampered with, or tinkered with again, locked and sealed under a presidential lock, and safe keeping, away from regulators and lobbyist.

President Barack Obama must do the following

(1) Reinstate the uptick rule .
(2) Remove mark-to-market accounting and replace it
with historic cost accounting.
(3) Dismantle and discontinue trading on all the short
ETFs, also called leveraged inverse ETFs.
(4) Reinstate the circuit breakers and trading curb.
(5) Regulate the Hedge Funds just like you do mutual
funds and pension funds.
(6) Regulate speculation on crude oil futures by
banning margin and leveraging except for the airline
industry or any other end user that can actually take
delivery of the commodity.
(7) Reduce interest rate for residential home mortgages
to 3.5% for every American. Including the so called
rich people with jumbo loans, they are Americans
too.

If Barack Obama fails to do the right thing, and fails to
implement the above mentioned 7-point actions plan solution
to solving this economic crisis. The Republicans should do so.

This book gives the explanation for what went wrong. The only
truth about what caused the economic crisis. The role of
Christopher Cox in destroying the Republican Party and the
solution for the Republican party to make a come back. The
Republican party needs to follow the above mentioned 7-point
action plan solution for fixing the economic crisis.

The Republican party must confess the errors of Christopher
Cox, his regulatory mistakes at the security and exchange
commission, and promise to correct those mistakes by
implementing the above mentioned 7-point action plan
solution to solving the economic crisis, before the majority of
the voting population can completely trust them with the
economy, because right now, the crisis occurred on their
watch, and they do not have any explanation of what went
wrong. This book solves that problem. This book explains it
all. This book offers the explanation of what went wrong.